INSIDE A
GESTAPO
PRISON

Krystyna Wituska, 1938

INSIDE A

GESTAPO

PRISON

The Letters of Krystyna Wituska,
1942–1944

Edited and Translated by Irene Tomaszewski

Wayne State University Press   Detroit

Library of Congress Cataloging-in-Publication Data

Wituska, Krystyna, 1920–1944.
[Na granicy zycia i smierci—listy i grypsy wiezienne Krystyny Wituskiej.
English. Selections]
Inside a Gestapo prison : the letters of Krystyna Wituska, 1942–1944 /
edited and translated by Irene Tomaszewski.
p. cm.
English translation originally published by Véhicule Press in 1997
under the title: I Am First a Human Being.
Includes bibliographical references.
ISBN 0-8143-3294-3 (pbk. : alk. paper)
1. Wituska, Krystyna, 1920-1944—Correspondence. 2. World War,
1939–1945—Prisoners and prisons, German. 3. World War, 1939–1945—
Underground movements—Poland. 4. Prisoners of war—Germany—
Correspondence. 5. Prisoners of war—Poland—Correspondence.
6. World War, 1939–1945—Personal narratives, Polish. 7. Spies—
Poland—Correspondence. I. Tomaszewski, Irene. II. Title.
D805.G3W5713 2006
940.53'438092—dc22
2006002880

∞

Design and typeset by Maya Rhodes
Composed in Adobe Garamond Pro and Britannic Bold

For Maya and Elizabeth

CONTENTS

ACKNOWLEDGMENTS

There are many people to thank for making possible this new edition of the collected letters of Krystyna Wituska. I should like to begin by gratefully acknowledging the two archives in Warsaw for their permission to publish this new edition of Wituska's letters: the Gabinet Rękopisów Biblioteki Uniwersiteckiej (Manuscript Archives of the University of Warsaw Library) and the Biuro Udostępniania i Archiwizacji Dokumentów Instytutu Pamięci Narodowej—Komisji Ścigania Zbrodni przeciwko Narodowi Polskiemu (Archives of the Institute of National Memory—Commission for the Investigation of Crimes against the Polish Nation).

I would like to thank Professors Tamara Trojanowska (University of Toronto), Tom Napierkowski (University of Colorado), John Micgiel (Columbia), John Bukowczyk (Wayne State University), Thaddeus Gromada (Executive Director of the Polish Institute of Arts and Sciences in America), and Dr. Aldona Wos for voicing their support for this publication.

My thanks to Maureen Mroczek Morris and her father, Władysław Mroczek Morris; Zbigniew Malecki and the Polish Socio-cultural Foundation of Quebec; Janusz Mazur and the Dymny Foundation in Montreal; the Adam Mickiewicz Foundation in Toronto; Roman Zawadzki and Dr. Ted Polak in California; Tony Muszynski in Calgary and Wanda Muszynski in Montreal; and Les Kuczynski in Chicago for their support.

My friend Małgorzata Dzieduszycka has been, as always and despite the many demands on her time, extraordinarily helpful and enthusiastic. I can never thank her enough.

And finally, to my editor at WSUP, Carrie Downes, many thanks for both the careful attention she gave my manuscript and for sharing her admiration of Krystyna Wituska.

NOTES ON THE NEW EDITION

The Wituska collection in the Gabinet Rękopisów Biblioteki Uniwersiteckiej (Manuscript Archives of the University of Warsaw Library) contains Wituska's correspondence to her parents, Maria and Feliks Wituski; letters from German War Court (Reichskriegsgericht) officials to Wituska's parents; letters from Hedwig and Helga Grimpe to the Wituskis; and letters from Wituska's prison friends. This correspondence, now on microfilm, no. 13080, is itemized in volume 7 of the Catalog of the Manuscript Archives of the University of Warsaw Library. Wituska's correspondence with Helga Grimpe is housed in the archives of the Biuro Udostępniania i Archiwizacji Dokumentów Instytutu Pamięci Narodowej—Komisji Ścigania Zbrodni przeciwko Narodowi Polskiemu (Archives of the Institute of National Memory—Commission for the Investigation of Crimes against the Polish Nation) collection "Ob," sygn. 334.

As in the original Canadian edition, the English translation of Krystyna Wituska's letters and some of the historical background for this book are based on Wanda Kiedrzyńska's 1970 book, *Na Granicy Życia i Śmierci, Listy i Grypsy Więzienne Krystyny Wituskiej* (Wanda Kiedrzyńska, editor, Państwowy Instytut Wydawniczy, Warsaw).

I was introduced to these letters by Wituska's cousin, Dr. Irena Bellert of Rawdon, Quebec. I am indebted to her for her reading of the translation, her suggestions and corrections, and for access to her letters from Wituska's fellow prisoner Maria Kacprzyk-Tabeau. Dr. Bellert also put me in touch with Wituska's nephew, Tomasz Steppa, the little "Kola" so frequently mentioned in the letters, who gave me photos and an unpublished memoir written by his mother, Halina (Krystyna's sister). These, together with his recollections of family history, provided me with a picture of life on his grandparents' estate before the war. For this, and for the warm hospitality of Tomasz and his wife, Basia, I am very grateful.

xi

A 1994 interview with Helga Grimpe in Germany provided further insights into the relationship between Krystyna and the compassionate and courageous Grimpe mother and daughter. I am indebted to Brian McKenna, director of the documentary film *A Web of War,* and Arnie Gelbart of Galafilm for access to this interview. The translation of the German prayer on the reverse side of Wituska's last letter, dated June 26, 1944, was translated by my friends Brian McCordick and Joan McCordick. Michał Bukojemski, of Warsaw, assisted with photos.

A brief description of the conditions imposed upon the Polish population under occupation by the German order has been added to the introduction. The information I have compiled is available in many standard works, including that of Norman Davies, Richard Lukas, and Adam Zamoyski. Fritz Arlt's comments on "population management" are taken from Götz Aly's and Susanne Heim's *Architects of Annihilation,* translated by A. G. Blunden (Princeton University Press, 2002). Alexander B. Rossino's *Hitler Strikes Poland* (University of Kansas Press, 2003) contains new insights on Nazi policies in occupied Poland, and *Praca Przymusowa Polaków w Trzeciej Rzeszy* (Forced Labor in the Third Reich) by Czesław Łukacz (Warsaw: Fundacja "Polsko-Niemieckie Pojednanie," 1999) provides important information about Polish slave labor in Germany. The passage by Jan Strzelecki, which I translated myself, is from a manuscript given to me by his friend, the late Andrzej Ziemilski.

I tried as much as possible to maintain the emotional nuances of Krystyna Wituska's letters, but English is a difficult language in which to express the many degrees of intimacy and affection that Polish permits. To avoid confusing the English-speaking reader, I refrained from using more than one form of a name, even though in Polish a variety of diminutives was used, each shedding light on the closeness of the relationship as well as the mood of the writer. The use of diminutives of nouns other than names also often reveals the mood of the writer, but there are no English equivalents. Adding the adjective "little" in each case would be both tiresome and imprecise. One notable exception is Wituska's sister, Halina, who is frequently addressed by the more affectionate form, Halinka. I have also retained the masculine or feminine form of Krystyna's family name, depending upon the individual.

These and some other interpretive liberties, notably in punctuation and use of idioms, have not, I hope, altered Wituska's own literary voice, one of the most distinctive I have encountered in any literature.

INTRODUCTION

In a letter dated October 3, 1943, Krystyna Wituska described the German atrocities in Poland as "cold-blooded genocide." Although the English word *genocide* was introduced only in 1944 by Raphael Lemkin, I did not hesitate to use it in translation. Wituska used the German word *Volksmord,* in Polish *ludobójstwo.* Both words had been in use long before the war, and, while not endowed with the full meaning Lemkin was to give it, the meaning went beyond "mass murder." The root word, *lud,* can mean "people" but also "nation." In one angry passage, Wituska specifically wrote about Poles and Jews; it is clear she meant not just the murder of *many* people but the murder of *a* people. Churchill, on the other hand, speaking at about the same time, was reduced to describing German atrocities in Poland as "the crime without a name."

Raphael Lemkin, an eminent Polish jurist who was one of the writers of the legal code when Poland regained its independence after World War I, could well have had *ludobójstwo* in mind when he coined the term *genocide,* but it is his definition of the word that has given the world a new concept and a new understanding of this crime. Although Lemkin had long been interested in studying the phenomenon of mass murder, what he witnessed in Poland before his escape propelled him into an intensive study of Nazi laws in various countries and their use against captive populations. He noted that beyond killing masses of people in order to take over their territory, Germany's intent was to target specific groups and their cultures for extinction. This could be done in a fairly short time by systematic killing, or it could be done slowly, driving a people to extinction through starvation, overwork, selective killing, and control of reproduction, while simultaneously attacking and dismantling their national, cultural, and religious symbols.

A single chapter on the German occupation would read like a litany of horrors. Of course there were horrors—many of them—and they

xiii

were not random acts of violence; rather, they were, as Lemkin noted, part of "a coordinated plan . . . aiming at the destruction of the foundations of life of national groups" by passing laws that attacked the "political and social institutions of culture, language, national feelings, religion and the economic existence of national groups, and the destruction of personal security, liberty, health, dignity and even the lives of individuals belonging to such groups."

Only later was it known that on August 22, 1939, Hitler gave the following instructions to his officers concerning the pending attack on Poland: "Kill Poles without mercy, all men, women and children of Polish descent or language. Only in this way can we obtain the living space we need. . . . The aim is elimination of living forces." In short, Germany wanted the land, not the people. Immediately after Poland's capitulation, Heinrich Himmler reiterated, "The removal of foreign races from the incorporated territories is one of the most essential goals to be accomplished in the German East."

The malevolent racial theories that rationalized the wanton cruelty of the German occupation forces often overshadow the Nazis' cold, pragmatic plan of conquest and colonization, but behind the raving racism and the brutish thuggery were the "four pillars" of National Socialism as identified by the German political scientist Franz Neumann: the Party, the military, the bureaucracy, and industry. A legion of colorless managers and advisers worked on economic plans for the Reich that included the appropriation of land as far as the Urals, the dispossession of Jews, Slavs, and other undesirables, the use of slave labor, and the annihilation of races deemed inferior, either through forced labor and starvation or by outright murder. All of this was justified in rational euphemisms: overpopulation, readjustment, restructuring, reconstruction, resettlement, and—particularly odious—the Generalgouvernement's "department of population management."

"Population management" began immediately in western Poland, which was incorporated into the Reich and subjected to complete Germanization. All place-names were changed, all Polish political, social, and cultural institutions were closed, all Poles were dismissed from their jobs, and all Polish schools were closed. Speaking Polish in public was forbidden. Thousands of Poles in prominent positions, or those simply from the middle and upper classes, were arrested and sent to the Dachau and Sachsenhausen concentration camps in Germany, and their families were evicted from their homes. Mass deportations of entire families followed. People were given one hour to pack and then were shipped in sealed freight cars to the Generalgouvernement, the central part of Poland controlled, but not annexed, by Germany. Once there, they had to fend for themselves, the lucky ones finding a room with relatives, others desperately trying to find something they could afford. Many were reduced to begging and to sleeping in any shelter they could find.

Many of the Jews in the annexed territories were also deported to the Generalgouvernement, but many more were confined in the ghetto in the city of Łódź, home to the second largest Jewish population in Poland. Set up in February 1940, the ghetto was completely sealed two months later, and overcrowding, hunger, and disease soon took their toll. Much of the city's Polish population had been expelled and replaced by Germans. The Jews were forced to use a special currency that was of no value outside the ghetto, so even smuggling, dangerous as it was, would have been useless. The situation was one of utter helplessness and hopelessness. The original inhabitants of the ghetto numbered about 140,000 Jews, but later, another 18,000 from smaller communities in the annexed territories, as well as thousands of Jews from Austria and Germany, were confined there. A small section of the ghetto was reserved for 5,000 Roma (gypsies). More than ninety factories, where the inmates made products ranging from army uniforms to armaments, were established in the ghetto. Paid in inadequate food rations and living in overcrowded squalor, more than 20 percent of the inmates died from starvation and disease. In 1943 the Germans began liquidating the ghetto, deporting to death camps first the aged, the sick, and the children, and finally all of the inmates, whether they were productive workers or not. By January 1945, fewer than 1,000 survivors were liberated out of a total ghetto population of 250,000.

This pattern, followed in virtually every city and throughout the countryside of Poland, ultimately led to a genocide that claimed the lives of 90 percent of the Jews in Poland and another three million transported from the occupied countries of Europe. It was, until then, an unimaginable crime, and despite many reports that reached the West, it was, perhaps because it was unimaginable, not believed until it was too late. Inside Poland, it was no secret; it was a crime committed in front of people who were themselves subjected to mass executions, mass arrests, and mass deportations—a daily regime of atrocities on an unprecedented scale.

The Poles who remained in the incorporated territories were kept only for menial labor. Pauperized, everyone was forced to work, including children over the age of twelve and subsequently children as young as eight. The Poles were subjected to humiliation and arbitrary acts of cruelty—not allowed to walk on the sidewalks, forced to doff their caps when passing a German, and subjected to blows or other punishments on the whim of any German. They were strictly segregated, relegated to the back of trams, denied entry to most commercial establishments, and barred from public parks.

The clergy in the incorporated territories was subjected to particularly harsh treatment. Polish Catholic churches, convents, and monasteries were closed. In the city of Poznań, twenty-eight churches and forty-five chapels were closed, leaving only two. In the larger city of Łódź, only four churches were left open. Many priests were killed in the early weeks of the occupation, and 500 were sent to Sachsenhausen. Of the rest, 80 percent were deported to the Generalgouvernement. Ultimately, the death rate for priests from the annexed territory was well over 30 percent. Nuns fared little better. Unlike any other part of occupied Europe, only in Poland were clergy of episcopal rank arrested and killed.

The Generalgouvernement, while not annexed, was nevertheless totally under German control. Not all policies were clearly stated at the beginning of the occupation, but ever more draconian laws were enacted in quick succession. It was clear from the start that no viable Polish state or Polish nation was meant to survive. Virtually every one of the conditions defined by Lemkin applied to the Generalgouvernement—even the name *Poland* was banned—as much as to the incorporated territories. The difference was really a matter of time, rather than of intent.

Immediately upon assuming control, the Germans began dismantling all signs of the Polish state and culture. Monuments, both national and cultural, were destroyed, museums and libraries were closed, and private and public art collections were stolen. Poles were barred from many public places and relegated to segregated buses. No political activity of any kind was permitted; indeed, political leaders at national, municipal, or any other level were among the first to be arrested, and many were executed. The destruction of archives, which was a deliberate attempt to eradicate all signs of Polish national existence, was one of the most serious war losses.

Polish churches in the Generalgouvernement, for the most part, remained open, though the clergy was frequently the target of repressive actions and gratuitous humiliation. By closing seminaries and forbidding the ordination of new priests, the Germans hoped that, with an accelerated death rate due to wartime conditions and without replacements, the clergy would wither away. As in other spheres of education, the church resorted to clandestine education of priests, among them the future pope, John Paul II, who studied with Archbishop Sapieha in Krakow.

Nuns received somewhat better treatment. Though arrested and executed in disproportionate numbers, they carried on with their prewar work, mainly in hospitals, orphanages, homes for the elderly, and schools. The Germans bombed hospitals clearly marked with red crosses during the opening battles of the war—subsequently murdering many patients—yet hospitals did continue functioning, albeit with insufficient staff and medical supplies. The orphanages had a greater role than ever to play. With so many parents arrested, deported, and killed, there was a great increase in the numbers of orphaned children. The nuns accepted all children without question, thereby providing a haven for many Jewish children. Despite regular checks by the Gestapo, there is no known case of Jewish children being discovered. In the eastern areas, nuns also took in Ukrainian children and, toward the end of the war, German children.

Priests and nuns took an active role in the underground, often offering their premises as meeting places and drop-off points and hiding members of the underground. One of the best known is the cloistered convent of the Carmelite nuns that regularly sheltered members of the Jewish Underground, provided them with a place to meet, and hid a cache of arms and ammunition in preparation for the uprising in the Warsaw Ghetto.

Theaters and concerts were strictly controlled, the music of Chopin completely banned. Most actors and musicians refused to perform in German productions, preferring instead to work in Polish-owned cafés and take part in clandestine performances. Cinemas, also under German control, restricted films to crude comedies and pornography. Publishing both books and periodicals was banned, and bookstores were closed. "The Polish lands are to be changed into a cultural desert," declared Hans Frank, the German governor of occupied Poland, as he implemented a policy intended to degrade Polish society by encouraging alcoholism, corruption, and collaboration. The underground, making a serious effort to persuade people to boycott German-controlled entertainment, organized clandestine cultural events and schools, secretly published newspapers and books, and operated social services to the greatest extent possible under such circumstances.

The attack on education was a major part of the German effort to suppress the possibility of Polish resistance. Not only were universities closed in the earliest stages of the occupation, but there was also a wholesale arrest of professors, most of whom were sent to the Sachsenhausen concentration camp in Germany. Those who managed to evade arrest continued teaching in underground universities, a dangerous undertaking for professors and students alike. One transport to the Stutthof concentration camp near Danzig included over 600 students who had been taking part in underground education.

Secondary schools were closed as well, the teachers and pupils in clandestine classes facing the same risks as their university counterparts. Elementary schools, while remaining open, were forced to restrict their curriculum to just enough rudimentary reading and arithmetic to prepare children to perform only simple tasks.

The assault on Poland's political, cultural, and educational leadership ultimately cost the nation 45 percent of its doctors and dentists (both Christian and Jewish), 57 percent of its lawyers, 15 percent of its teachers, 40 percent of its university professors, and 18 percent of the clergy. 4,000 priests were sent to concentration camps. They made up 65 percent of all clergy at Dachau and 85 percent of those killed. Only Polish clergy were used for medical experimentation.

Hitler, Himmler, and Hans Frank all referred to the Generalgouvernement at least once as nothing more than a "labor reserve." Dr. Fritz Arlt, the young director in charge of "population management," busied himself with statistics that provided him with euphemisms for his solutions to the problem of "overpopulation." Among other things, he supervised the hospitals where elderly and seriously ill patients were murdered in the first weeks of the occupation. He redesigned welfare distribution in a way that ensured it would not "be influenced solely by charitable and humanitarian considerations, when instead we should be guided constantly by the national and ethno-political interests of the German Reich." Bearing in mind Himmler's policy of "fomenting strife between the different ethnic groups," Arlt found that distributing welfare benefits according to racial criteria served this purpose very well. As for the general reduction of the non-German population, Arlt noted with satisfaction that "the thousands of war casualties have already made inroads in the population numbers."

Until the attack on the Soviet Union in June 1941, the Germans treated the Jews with contempt, committed endless acts of gratuitous brutality, and confined them in prison-like ghettos. But, in some respects, the danger to Poles during this early period seemed greater. Mass executions of Poles had been a regular occurrence, as were public executions. People were hanged on makeshift gallows, from city lampposts, and from balconies of public buildings; they were shot by firing squad in city parks or in front of churches, taken in trucks to secret executions, and casually shot on city streets. Orchestras were sometimes ordered to play to drown out the wails of the helpless bystanders.

But with the German advance into the east came the mass slaughter of Jews—first in the smaller towns, while the ghettos that were established in the bigger ones were liquidated soon after. Then, in January 1942, at a meeting in Wannsee, Nazi leaders decided on the unprecedented plan to annihilate the entire Jewish population of Europe. Establishing death camps such as Treblinka and Birkenau, they began their murderous campaign with industrial efficiency. As for Poland in general, Hans Frank noted with satisfaction that the measures in place had already reduced the population and that with conditions so unfavorable to the birthrate, it would not be long before the problem took care of itself. As he put it: "Finis Poloniae."

Despite—or perhaps because of—the awful terror, Poles resisted, and the Generalgouvernement, besides being a "labor reserve," also became an immense prison. As early as June 1940, the SS and the police district command had reported that due to the intensification of Polish resistance there were not enough prisons in all of Poland to hold all their prisoners. Himmler therefore ordered the construction of Auschwitz, which was built not in the Generalgouvernement but in the incorporated territories—that is, within Germany.

For almost two years, Poles comprised the main group of prisoners in Auschwitz, ultimately 150,000, half of whom perished. (The death camp in the Auschwitz complex, Birkenau, was set up in 1942.) As part of a "pacification" and German settlement program in the Zamość region, 100,000 Poles were deported to Majdanek, where half of them perished. Poles constituted the largest number of prisoners in almost all the camps in the Reich and in occupied Poland. To list just the largest ones: 40,000 in Mauthausen, 35,000 in Dachau, 30,000 in Sachsenhausen, 23,000 in Buchenwald, 16,000 in Plaschau, and 34,000 in Ravensbruck, the women's concentration camp where Polish prisoners were subjected to medical experimentation. Finally, the Germans set up three special concentration camps for children. The biggest one, in Łódź, confined 13,000 children, 12,000 of whom perished.

Much larger groups were deported as forced laborers to Germany. The largest proportion of Polish laborers, 60 percent, worked on farms and the balance in various industries and as domestic servants. The first transport of slave labor took place in September 1939, though street roundups began in earnest in 1940. The Germans also tried to entice volunteers, but, despite the widespread impoverishment of the population, their campaign failed. In fact, by the time of the last conscription of forced laborers in 1945, out of 2.8 million Polish workers in Germany, only a few thousand were volunteers, some attracted by (false) promises of good wages and working conditions, others to escape the attention of the Gestapo. The last group included Jews who, carrying false identity papers, got a measure of security by being officially classed as Poles.

In the Reich, as in the Generalgouvernement, the treatment of Poles was in line with official Nazi ideology of their value being determined by their capacity for work. Goebbels expressed the view that working prisoners to death was an excellent policy in that it liquidated the population and got some benefit from them in the process.

The status of Polish workers in the Reich was at the bottom of the scale, on par with that of Russians. Deprived of all human rights, they were subject to the whims first of the Gestapo and then of their employers. Arbitrary punishment by Germans, with no appeal, was a daily reality. Poles who struck back at a German or were suspected of sabotage or underground activities were subject to summary execution by the Gestapo. Indicative of the racial attitudes of the Nazis was the obsession with, and penalty for, real or alleged sexual relations with a German. An accusation was enough to condemn Poles to summary execution, which in cases of "sexual crimes" usually meant a public execution witnessed by Gestapo and party officials, German bystanders, and Poles—ostensibly to serve as a deterrent. Often these victims were very young men.

There were also some instances when both a Pole and a German were executed because they actually had established a relationship.

In the early part of the war, mothers of young children were not deported for labor unless they were accused of a crime against the Reich. This too eventually changed as the demand for labor in Germany grew. Children born to Polish women in Germany were taken away and either killed or given to Germans for adoption. Many women, whether in labor camps or living on farms or in private households, tried to hide their babies, occasionally with success.

In sum, 2,826,500 Poles were deported as slave labor, of which women comprised 23 percent in 1941 and, by July 1944, 34.5 percent. Some children used as slave laborers were as young as ten. Poles comprised 60 percent of all foreign workers in Germany, supplying agricultural and domestic labor and at least 495 German industrial firms. A further 23,000 Poles were sent to work in France.

At the same time, Polish resistance surpassed that of any occupied country, and, as noted by historian John Keegan, Poland "produced few collaborators and no puppet chief, a unique distinction in the European response to German aggression." Before capitulating to the Germans in October 1939, the Polish commanders ordered their troops to go underground. The Armia Krajowa (Home Army) eventually counted 380,000 sworn resistance fighters. The civil administration also went underground, maintaining a secret educational system, justice system, and other functions. The Poles rightly refer to this as "The Underground State."

The Polish resistance was indeed prodigious. Between January 1941 and the Warsaw Uprising in 1944, the Home Army damaged over 6,900 locomotives; destroyed almost 1,000 railway trucks and damaged another 20,000; set 450 transports on fire; damaged or destroyed over 4,000 military vehicles; destroyed 1,100 petrol tanks; destroyed 4,674 tons of petrol; destroyed 3 oil wells; destroyed 122 military warehouses; burned 8 military food storage depots; burned 15 factories and otherwise incapacitated 7 others; disabled or destroyed almost 100 aircraft; and blew up 39 railway bridges. German records show that the Polish underground stopped one in eight Wehrmacht (German army) transports from reaching the eastern front.

In 1942 a group of underground activists who were engaged in helping Jews survive outside the ghettos organized the Council for Aid to Jews in an attempt to coordinate their efforts and provide moral, financial, and logistical assistance to people involved in this dangerous undertaking. Code-named *Zegota*, the council enlisted the help of the Home Army and received financial assistance via airdrops from the Government in Exile in London.

Although the war, and the resistance, continued for another full year, the Warsaw Uprising of August 1944 was the culmination of Polish resistance both in the determination of the Polish fighters and in the ferocity of the Germans. Addressing district commanders and commanders of military colleges, on September 21, 1944, Himmler stated, "This is the fiercest of all our battles since the start of the war. It compares to the street battles of Stalingrad. . . . We will finish this in the next five to six weeks. Then we will have destroyed Warsaw, the capital, the heart, the flower of the intelligentsia of the former . . . Polish nation; this nation that for 700 years has blocked our road to the East and stood always in our way since the first battle at Tannenberg."

At a conference of SS officers on October 17, 1944, he added, "The city must completely disappear from the surface of the earth and serve only as a transport station for the Wehrmacht. No stone can remain standing. Every building is to be razed to its foundation."

At the end of the war, the Poles were left with a country devastated like no other. The losses were staggering, including 30 percent of all residential buildings, 43 percent of cultural collections, 60 percent of all schools, 55 percent of all health services, 60 percent of all public buildings, and 56 percent of transport and communications infrastructure, not to mention personal possessions such as furniture, china, silverware, pianos, and photograph albums.

But those were material losses. The human destruction was unprecedented, with nearly two million dead at the hands of the Nazis. The surviving population was traumatized, their physical condition appalling. The survivors suffered from tuberculosis, heart disease, circulation problems, arthritis, rheumatism, and psychological disorders; children had rickets and a host of other developmental problems. The educated elite—the leadership and the professions, the ranks of teachers and students—was gutted, and the young lost, or had severely curtailed, six years of education. There were very few facilities to tend the sick and the maimed.

Families waited for fathers and mothers, sons and daughters to return from the camps and prisons or wherever they had been deported. But millions did not return. Some remained prisoners in the Soviet Union, others refused to return from the West. Most Jewish survivors found no one at all: no family members, no friends, and no neighbors had survived. And, as planned by the Nazis, for six years there were almost no births.

This introduction, intended as a background for Krystyna Wituska's story, concentrates on the occupation of Poland and its impact on the Polish Christian population and the Polish state. The genocide of the Jews, however, is an intrinsic part of this tragic period in Poland's history. There are many excellent works on this subject and a cursory glance here would serve no purpose. However, the following quotation from a memoir written by Jan Strzelecki, a Polish sociologist who was a student in the underground university and also a member of the resistance, is an eloquent evocation of the parallel tragedies of the Poles and the Jews and of the singular nature of the Jewish genocide.

> Our existence bordered on that of the prisoners, the two were interchangeable, their existence was our shadow . . . the world of slaves was not an exotic world to us; it remained a constant possibility . . . the distance that in a teenage imagination was that of centuries, of epochs . . . that distance was now reduced to blind chance. It was only by chance that we did not work in the quarries where the mortality rate was higher than that in the quarries of the Peloponnesus. That distance, of centuries of European history, was reduced to nothing, and this phenomenon struck us with great wonder. In the face of our experience . . . the history of modern times was the opposite of all theories of progress. . . . We had a deep affinity with the fate of slaughtered races, with peoples taken into bondage, with inhabitants of cities destroyed by flames, and with devastated countries.
>
> The evil around us . . . could not be relieved by any historical explanation. . . . The evil was in the guise of pride derived from the destruction of life, it was the personification of cruelty experienced as absolute power over the existence of another person. The prime symbol of that evil was the wall that stood in our city. The wall stood for the gradual

death of people who happened to be Jews. Their suffering was the fulfillment of absolute evil. . . . The world of the condemned and the world of the condemner were ideally separated. Not a single sign, not a child's cry, a young girl's beauty, a mother's cry, nothing penetrated to the outside world.

"Genocide, as a word, turns on a genocidal intention," noted Michael Ignatieff in a lecture at the Holocaust Museum in Washington, discussing Raphael Lemkin's word and its relation to Poland. The word has no meaning unless it can be connected to a "clear intention to exterminate a human group, in whole or in part." Lemkin saw that intent in Germany's plan for Poland.

This was the setting in which nineteen-year-old Krystyna Wituska found herself at the time of her arrest. A harsh reality that clashed with the natural hopes of youth, it was a world of barbarism, a world of slaves and omnipotent masters. "For several years we lived on the fringes of the final test," wrote Jan Strzelecki. "Would I endure this? Would I turn out to be nothing but flesh? The flesh was frail; it was something that would quickly beg for mercy . . . in obedience to the tormentors."

Nothing in Krystyna Wituska's young life could have prepared her for the trial that awaited her. A privileged child of the landed gentry, she grew up on a large estate in western Poland, an area known as Wartheland, where her father, an agronomist, raised sugar beets for export. In an unpublished memoir, Krystyna's older sister, Halina, described a family life with doting parents, high-spirited, fun-loving girls, a wide circle of friends, and a strong emphasis on education.

The early education of the sisters was in the hands of governesses, the first one emphasizing languages, particularly French, followed by others who prepared them for high school at a convent in Poznań. The girls enjoyed the freedom of country life—running barefoot all summer, climbing trees, swimming, and, a special treat, accompanying their father on rounds of the estate. They had their own "zoological garden" where they kept a variety of birds, insects, snakes, and other small animals that they sometimes used mischievously in merciless pranks on their unsuspecting urban governesses.

Boarding at the convent was accepted as a necessity rather than a delight, and the sisters always looked forward to their long holidays,

Krystyna (clutching her father's leg) and her sister, Halina,
on the Wituski estate

often with friends and extended family visiting. As they grew older, house parties, overnight bicycle tours, and camping filled out the young people's social life.

After high school, Halina went on to further study in horticulture, but Krystyna, suffering from a respiratory illness, possibly incipient tuberculosis, was sent to a private school in Switzerland in the hope that the fresh mountain air would be therapeutic. Just before she left, Krystyna was engaged to a childhood friend, Zbyszek Walc—the son of Drs. Wanda and Lucjan Walc, who owned a well-known private medical clinic in Warsaw. Zbyszek continued his studies at the University of Warsaw.

As the summer of 1939 approached and the threat of war increased, Krystyna begged her family to let her come home. They tried to persuade her to stay in Switzerland until she was stronger, but Krystyna was insistent. She couldn't bear the anxiety of staying away from her family at a time like this. Reluctantly, they gave in to their willful daughter; no one at the time could imagine that this would be a war like no other. She came home in July. By that time, her father, a reserve officer, and Zbyszek, a cadet officer, had already been mobilized. Krystyna and Zbyszek exchanged letters, optimistically hoping to be together again soon.

The German attack on September 1, 1939, was swift and brutal. On September 17, their Soviet allies fulfilled their secret agreement and attacked from the east. The Wituski women followed the news on the radio, but before long these broadcasts became irregular and eventually ceased altogether. They heard nothing from Feliks Wituski until he arrived home shortly after Poland's capitulation on October 5. It would be another month or so before they would get news that Zbyszek had been taken prisoner.

For a short time, the Wituski estate, isolated from the main roads, was left in peace. The family took in passing refugees, among them a young man from Gdansk (Danzig), Janusz Steppa, whose stories about the fighting on the front were disquieting. They passed the time in an eerie calm, the sisters even taking German lessons from Steppa. Then, in December 1939, the calm was broken with the arrival of German patrols. The Wituskis were given fifteen minutes to pack, trucked to waiting trains, and deported to the Generalgouvernement. Krystyna's childhood home was now in German territory.

Dumped inside the Generalgouvernement border, the deportees

were left to fend for themselves. The bitter cold, the lack of food, and the unsanitary conditions in the trains claimed hundreds of victims; many died, many more were in physical or psychological distress. It was at this point that Krystyna and her sister discovered that their parents' marriage had been an unhappy one, held together by agreement until the girls married. Without a home to sustain them, the Wituski family split up. Krystyna and her mother headed for Warsaw, finding food and shelter among strangers along the way, where they ultimately moved in with relatives; her father set off to find work on an estate expropriated by the Germans, while Halina and the young Janusz Steppa had, it was revealed, fallen in love. The two young people set off to find shelter on their own.

In Warsaw, Krystyna first shared a room with a young aunt, Alina, whose husband had been killed in the first months of the war. She later moved in with her mother, who had rented a room in the home of some Warsaw friends. Alina, who ran a small shop where Poles could buy provisions with ration coupons, got Krystyna a job in the stockroom.

It was while working here that Krystyna ran into Karol Szapiro, a young man she had met when both were temporarily sheltered in a church on their way to Warsaw. References to Karol Szapiro, a Jewish student who had escaped from Łódź with his family and was living under an assumed name with forged documents, were guarded. She never wrote to him directly but often referred to him as her "old tutor." In a 1996 letter to Krystyna's cousin, a prison friend wrote that it was Karol whom Krystyna loved, and that her engagement to her childhood friend, Zbyszek, was just a fond memory from her youth. Karol was shot and killed at a railway station, possibly because his identity was discovered. Krystyna's parents withheld this information from her, writing only that he was "missing."

It seems that Krystyna got involved in the resistance quite early: it is known that she was involved in the ZWZ (the Union for Armed Resistance), a precursor to the Home Army, which took in all but the extreme right and left under its leadership. By her own admission, she was initially attracted by the excitement of resistance and defiance. But youthful bravado is short-lived. Another contemporary, Aleksander Gieysztor, wrote, "Only the young have courage. With maturity, the best you can hope for is the mastery of fear." Maturity came quickly during the occupation.

Krystyna's role in the underground was minor. Assigned to an espionage cell, she was to mingle with German officers at cafés and engage in conversation about the location of certain squadrons, the strength of battalions, and the names of officers. This was not top-secret information, and Krystyna was a very low-level spy. In fact, at one point a German officer told her he knew what she was doing but would not report her if she stopped immediately. She stopped, but temporarily. In June 1942 the underground suspected she was being watched, so she left Warsaw for a while. When she returned, she was assigned to a new cell that included two other students, Maria (Marysia) Kacprzyk and Wanda Kamińska. Before long, she was arrested. Searching Krystyna's room, the Gestapo found the names and addresses of her two colleagues, and they were arrested the following night.

Krystyna was taken to Pawiak, the main prison in Warsaw, and was interrogated at Aleja Szucha, the notorious interrogation center in the Gestapo headquarters. It is not known how severe her interrogations were, but the Gestapo obviously believed she knew more than she revealed. On October 22, 1942, she was transported to the military prison Alexanderplatz in Berlin. With her were three other Polish women, including Cezara Dickstein, an older woman and family friend to whom Krystyna referred as her "prison mother" those first few weeks, and Olga Jędrkiewicz, the cheerful "Olenka," who would later share cell #18 with Krystyna at Alt-Moabit Prison.

During her interrogations in Berlin, she realized that Zbyszek had also been brought there and that their arrests were somehow related. Captured on October 25, 1939, as a prisoner of war, Zbyszek was first sent to the Itzehoe camp and then to Stalag II Neubrandenburg. In March 1942 he was removed from the POW camps and sent to work for German companies as a slave laborer. This was against the Geneva Convention but frequently the fate of Polish POWs in Nazi Germany. Zbyszek linked up with a Polish prisoners' underground network that supplied information to the Polish government about the treatment of prisoners. One of his reports was intercepted. In a search of Zbyszek's belongings, the Gestapo found Krystyna's address. It was this, rather than her own underground activities, that led to her arrest.

It was at the "Alex," as she later called Alexanderplatz, that Krystyna met her most beloved friend, Maria (Mimi) Terwiel, with whom she shared a cell for several weeks. Mimi, ten years older than Krystyna, was a German dissident, a lawyer who, together with her fiancé, Hans Helmut Himpel, belonged to the Schulze-Boysen/Harnack Organization Rote Kapelle. This was a Soviet-backed espionage organization set up in all German-occupied countries; in Germany it attracted opponents of the regime who had few other resources for organized resistance. The Gestapo cracked the Rote Kapelle in 1942, arrested its members, and destroyed most of its records. A Gestapo document dated December 29, 1942, revealed that half of the membership were women and young girls. According to their fellow prisoners, Mimi and Hans were Social Democrats, not Communists, and it is doubtful that Mimi realized the full extent of the organization's activities.

In February 1943 Krystyna was transferred to the Alt-Moabit prison, where some of the conditions, such as food and hygiene, were a bit better, but overall it was harsher, and for the first few months Krystyna was in solitary confinement. She was given a sewing machine and was forced to work all day, stopping only for one meal.

At Alt-Moabit, the prisoners underwent further interrogation and were then put on trial, a parody of justice staged to maintain the impression that the Nazis continued to respect the legal system. After the trials, and pending ratification of the sentences—death in most cases—prisoners were taken out of solitary, though they were still obliged to work, sewing dresses, blouses, and purses for German civilians. Krystyna, along with her new cell mates, Monika Dymska and Olenka Jędrkiewicz, was condemned to death.

Their sentences came as no surprise. At the end of 1942, after the German defeat at Stalingrad, Hitler ordered a mandatory death sentence for all spies and communists, and only those prisoners held on lesser charges got terms in penal or concentration camps. Still, the *drei Polen Kinder* (three Polish children), as Mimi called the trio in cell #18, appealed their sentences, hoping to be included in an amnesty proclaimed by Hitler in 1943 to mark the tenth anniversary of the Nazis' election to power.

While Krystyna waited for the decision on her appeal, one by one, her friends' lives were settled. Parting with friends was the most painful part of prison life for Krystyna. She was overjoyed when Marysia Kacprzyk and Wanda Kamińska were spared, especially because she felt partly responsible for their arrest, their addresses having been found at her place. Marysia wrote to another friend, "Krystyna was extremely happy that her friends had been spared the death penalty. After the trial, she hugged and kissed us with tears of joy in her eyes. She behaved as though her own verdict were unimportant. No sign of despair, sadness, or regret. She proudly and very sincerely showed her happiness that her friends' lives were saved. You could see that it affected the Germans. I was proud of her and very impressed."

Mimi and Helmut, being linked to a communist organization, had no chance of reprieve. In March 1943 two other prisoners, Wiesława Jezierska and Olga Kamińska, were executed. They had both worked with a Polish-Yugoslav unit that escorted British POWs south across the Bulgarian-Turkish border after helping them escape from Kazamat Fortu VII, an old, windowless, fortress-like Prussian prison in Poznań. Olga and Wiesława were caught on the Serb-Bulgarian border in the company of two British officers identified only by their surnames, Sinclair and Littledale. Olga was married to a young Pole who was trying to get to Palestine to join the Polish forces there but was caught when the Germans entered Yugoslavia. Because Olga was pregnant, she was kept in a Belgrade prison until she gave birth, after which her son was sent to a *Kinderheim* (an orphanage) and she to Alt-Moabit. Because of her son, she had asked for clemency but was denied. She managed to get word to her parents about the boy, and they eventually recovered him.

Not much is known about the Poles who were sent to prison in Berlin. Few survived, fewer still left memoirs. Most just disappeared, last seen in the hands of the Gestapo in Poland and not heard from again. Sometimes a formal notice of execution was received by the families. Krystyna Wituska's letters offer a rare glimpse into that dark world.

We owe the existence of most of these letters to one of Krystyna's prison guards, Hedwig Grimpe. Mrs. Grimpe had not volunteered for this job but had been assigned to it, and at times, her daughter said in a 1994 interview, she found it almost unbearable. Her presence at Moabit, however, was a great comfort to the condemned. She was good to all prisoners but developed a special fondness for Krystyna and the other Polish women.

When Mrs. Grimpe was on duty, the prisoners could let down their guard, relax, and talk freely. She chatted with them, comforted them, and brought them food, writing paper and pencils, and anything else that was possible. She kept them informed about political events and military news. During air raids on Berlin, when all other guards went down to the shelters, Mrs. Grimpe stayed behind to reassure the prisoners that they would not be trapped there.

Perhaps her greatest contribution to their emotional well-being was that she enabled them to communicate with one another by delivering notes from one cell to another, and occasionally even sent some letters to their families, thereby circumventing the prison censor. All this she did at great risk, and, most remarkable of all, she involved her sixteen-year-old daughter, Helga, in these acts of kindness.

Helga became a friend, a pen pal, whose letters brought a glimpse of the outside world to the prisoners, and someone to whom they could write candidly, sometimes expressing their pain and their anger, other times discussing poetry and exchanging youthful humor. At Krystyna's request, Helga copied out poetry for her—her favorites were Schiller and Goethe. These letters, between a teenage daughter of a German prison guard and a young prisoner from the Polish resistance, must rank among the most unusual of prison correspondences. After Krystyna's closest prison friend, the German dissident Mimi Terwiel, was executed, Mrs. Grimpe established contact between Krystyna and Mimi's brother and sister, smuggling their letters into and out of Moabit.

The prisoners loved Hedwig Grimpe, whom they called *Sonnenschein* (Sunshine). Krystyna wrote to Helga about Mrs. Grimpe's appearance at the door during an air raid, how she held her and comforted her. For those few minutes, Krystyna felt she was in her own mother's arms. "Are you angry," she wrote, "that I stole your mother for this moment?"

Death was a steady companion to these prisoners. Every Wednesday, the inmates would be selected and taken away the next day, first to Barnimstrasse, an administration center from which prisoners from throughout Berlin were processed for their next destination: forced labor, another prison, a labor camp, a penal camp, a concentration camp, or execution. The condemned were then taken to Plotzensee, where they were beheaded.

Interviewed in Germany in 1994, Helga recalled one time when her mother had to escort a young girl to her execution. She came home that day trembling and crying that she could not go on. This must have been after the execution of Krystyna's friend Wanda Węgierska. Before the prisoners were escorted to the guillotine, the guard had to cut their hair. Wanda told Krystyna that she would ask that her hairpins be brought back to her. Krystyna writes in one letter about a tearful Sonnenschein coming to her cell bearing Wanda's hairpins. Helga also recalled the Polish women's concern for her mother's safety. On one occasion when she delivered a letter to Krystyna's cell, another guard suddenly appeared at the door. One of the girls—Helga did not remember which one—immediately stuffed it in her mouth and ate it to protect their beloved Sonnenschein.

It is hard to understand why Krystyna's execution was delayed so long—almost fifteen months after her sentence was passed. During that time, she went to bed every Tuesday wondering whether the next day it would be her turn. "Another Wednesday has passed," she would write to Helga. "I'm still alive."

In December 1943 Krystyna was transferred to a prison in Halle-Saale. Without Sonnenschein to transmit secret notes and no friends there who survived, little is known about her stay there. A German prisoner reported after the war that Krystyna was mostly in a solitary cell, and until May 1944, she was usually handcuffed. Her letters are few and quite formal. All had to pass the censor. Life there was obviously harsh, and she especially missed the companionship of Polish prisoners. Her physical condition deteriorated. In a poignant letter, she asked Zbyszek's mother, Dr. Wanda Walc, a dermatologist, if she had a remedy for her hair, which was falling out. She described herself as a "plucked chicken," said that she would remain vain until the last moment, and asked for some good shampoo.

The letters to her parents from Halle-Saale, as those before from Alexanderplatz and Alt-Moabit, are characterized by her overriding concern for her parents. She believed that her ordeal caused greater torment for them than it did for her. In this regard, her letters reveal a concern expressed in the prison letters of many young prisoners, both under the Germans and later the Soviets, of which there are many in archives in Poland and elsewhere in Europe. In my many interviews with survivors of the war, the most frequent expression of sorrow is about the suffering of mothers. Krystyna is no exception. Her parting words to her mother are, "When you smile, I smile with you, but when you cry, I cry with you," and she exhorts her mother to hold her head high and to have courage, no matter what.

For the sake of her parents, Krystyna expressed hope, or at least acceptance and serenity. In the next-to-last letter she wrote at Halle-Saale, she briefly entertains a futile hope that her father might be allowed one more visit and, with unexpected, spontaneous candor, she writes, "I think that unlike last year, this time there would be no need to keep up appearances while deep inside we querulously wonder: 'Will we ever see one another again?'" Then, without a break, she thanked him for the hairbrush she just received.

Hundreds of Poles passed through Moabit, as did hundreds from other countries. Krystyna was just one of them, unique as every human is unique. Most died leaving no trace of their agony. Krystyna's letters are a memorial to them all. The official ones were preserved by her parents; the others were delivered to the Wituskis by Mrs. Hedwig Grimpe after the war. The teenage Helga collected hers in an album that she titled the *Kleeblattalbum* (Cloverleaf album), so named for the cloverleaf signature Krystyna, Olenka, and Monika used, each of the three petals representing each of them. Gerd and Ursel Terwiel, Mimi's brother and sister, forwarded some others to Wanda Kiedrzyńska, a historian and survivor of Ravensbruck, who first published the collection in Poland.

Finally there was Hedwig Grimpe's letter to Krystyna's parents in 1946. "I can only assure you without exaggeration what happiness I felt reading your first words to me. You lifted from me a very heavy burden." We can only surmise what the Wituskis might have said to Mrs. Grimpe, but no doubt it would have been in the spirit expressed by Krystyna when she wrote, "I am first a human being, and only then a Pole." The Grimpes also were, first and foremost, human beings.

Krystyna explained that it was easier to face death believing that she would die for justice and for all humanity, and not just for her own people. With that belief, she reached the universal. She belongs to us all.

Alexanderplatz Prison, Berlin
November 12, 1942

Dearest Mummy,

Don't cry—I am well, in good spirits, and doing fine. Things are going well. Please send me the following things: my red dress, a woolen skirt, warm underwear and stockings, a warm nightie, needles and thread, and warm slippers.

Dear Father, I beg of you, take care of Mummy. She's so alone now.[1] Please write to me often.

And send me some laundry soap and toothpaste. I think about you all the time. I kiss you, dearest Mummy, and Father, a thousand times.

My address: Berlin
Polizei Gefangnis Alexanderplatz
Frauenstation V

Alexanderplatz Prison, Berlin
December 22, 1942

Dear parents,

It's almost Christmas! I send you all my best wishes, and I am sure that we all have the same great wish—that someday we will be together again. I'll be thinking about you all on Christmas Day. I received two little packages from Father as well as your letters, Mummy, with all their good wishes for Christmas. I felt so happy! I want to assure you, Mummy, that I am in good health; please don't worry about me. I haven't lost weight; I haven't even had a cold. A prison doctor examined me and said my lungs are clear.[2] The slacks are wonderfully warm. The

---

1. When Krystyna's parents were evicted from their home by the German army, they finally ended their disciplined but unhappy marriage. For Krystyna, the fact that her mother was alone in these circumstances was a continuous source of anguish.

2. Krystyna had borderline tuberculosis before the war.

prison here has central heating, and the food is much better than it was in the Warsaw prison. I can honestly say that they are polite and considerate. There is nothing to do here, though I sometimes get books or newspapers to read. We are two in the cell so I have company. My cell mate—a young German[3]—is very nice and friendly. We pass the time well enough. Since we have no lights after dark, we go to bed early.

I am very pleased that Halina[4] and her little one are well and that Janek[5] is feeling better. Please send my best wishes to Pani Walc[6] and all her family. Please, Mummy, I want you to remain cheerful and calm. We can't, after all, undo fate. I am certain we will see one another again, and then I want to see you composed and in good spirits. I am very grateful to the Mierkowskis[7] for being so kind and pleasant. Don't worry if, in the future, I write to you less frequently. I have special permission to write three letters; that is exceptional during the interrogation period.

Please, Father, write to me and tell me how things are going on the Brwinów estate. Do you enjoy your work as much as ever?[8] Best wishes to all our friends for Christmas, and kisses to all.

Your Tina

Please send me a couple of twelve-pfennig stamps. Our friends in Königsberg can get them for you.

---

3. Rosemarie (Mimi) Terwiel, a German dissident, who became Krystyna's closest friend.

4. Krystyna's sister.

5. Krystyna's brother-in-law.

6. Dr. Wanda Walc, the mother of Krystyna's fiancé, Zbyszek (who was taken to a POW camp in the fall of 1939 and had not been heard from). She will usually refer to Dr. Walc as Pani Wanda—deferential but less formal than Dr. or Pani Walc. (*Pani* is not quite the equivalent of *Mrs.*; it is more like the French *Madame*.)

7. Friends of the Wituskis in Warsaw, from whom Krystyna's mother had rented a room.

8. Her father, an agronomist, was working on an estate in the central part of Poland, known as the Generalgouvernement during the occupation.

Alexanderplatz, Berlin
January 1, 1943

Dear parents,

The day before yesterday I was overwhelmed with joy. I received a big parcel full of warm things as well as a little package from you, Father. How did you spend Christmas? My cell mate and I spent it quite pleasantly. On Christmas Eve she received a great package from home with so many good things in it, we simply didn't know what to eat first. What's more, we had candlelight and two cigarettes. I must say, things haven't been that good in a long time. I wish you all the best for the New Year. Keep well and write often.

Things are still pretty good with me. I exercise every morning, I get something to read during the day, and we talk a lot; so it's good, all things considered—I've adapted to my situation.

Tell Halina that I'd like her to write to me about everything—especially about little Kola.[9] How I'd love to get a photo of him. Have you any news about Zbyszek? I am living in the middle of Berlin and will soon be an old timer here, but I still haven't seen the city. I am making progress in German, as you can tell by these letters. I am so pleased you get together with Dr. Walc quite often. She's so clever and courageous. I've always admired her.

Dear Father, why do you write so infrequently? I get mail often from Mummy, but I long for news from you too.

Dearest Mummy, don't write such sad letters. Be an optimist, like me, and think only about our happiness when we are finally together again. I hope you believe this as strongly as I do. Again, I send you my best wishes for the New Year. Keep well, write to me as often as possible with lots of good news. Lots of kisses.

Your Tina

---

9. Krystyna's nephew.

Alexanderplatz, Berlin
January 19, 1943

Dear parents,

Thank you so much for your letters and parcels. I got the postage stamps and also those warm things you sent me. Now, dear Mummy, I'm not freezing anymore. The parcels from Father always please me and they are so useful. Are you both well? Are you very sad, Mother? I often feel guilty that because of me you are so unhappy. Don't be angry with me, dear Mummy, and try to forget about the times when I wasn't as good toward you as I should have been. I'm sorry.

Daddy, I'm sorry you have such problems at Brwinów and hope that things will get better. I do hope you can stay there. I have such fond memories of that place and love it so. I am well but sometimes, when I think about old times, I get sad. It is very comforting, dear Mummy, to know that you pray for me. Perhaps your prayers will not be in vain.

We cut out a beautiful cross out of cardboard, and we've hung it on the window. It looks so lovely when the sun is rising and at night when the stars are shining. Often we sit and gaze out the window at the night sky for hours. We tell each other stories and tales, and so we pass the time until, at last, sleep overcomes us and we go to bed. I think often about Zbyszek, and I am sure his future will be bright. If you know where he is, send him the same things you've sent me. I'm sure he needs them.

Dearest Mummy, give my best wishes to Pani Wanda and tell her not to lose courage. Write to me a lot and often. And give my best regards to the Mierkowskis.

My darling sister, I hope that your family is all together, well, and happy. How I'd love to see your little one. No doubt he is getting big and strong. Can you send me his photograph? I am so happy to think that you are together with your husband and child, living peacefully and quietly, away from life's cares. Sometimes I am jealous of you, Halinka, but I suppose I must bear my misfortune bravely.

I have one great worry, and I ask your help. Please don't leave Mother alone. She is so lonely now. Be good to her. Could you not keep her with you if I must stay here much longer? Spare me this worry. Think how alone she must feel. It hurts me so much. It's only now that I'm so far away from her that I realize how much I owe her and how I love her. I am sure you have long felt the same way and are doing everything you can to make her life a little easier.

Please raise your son in the spirit of peace. May he never be a soldier! War is so terrible and frightening.

Dear Halinka and Janek, I wish you all good things. How I'd love to be able to hold your little one and kiss him. Keep well! Love and kisses.

Tina

Alt-Moabit Prison, Berlin
February 14, 1943

My most beloved Mummy,

I received your card of the 30th. The parcels will probably be returned to you since they've moved me to another prison three days ago.

These past few days I've missed you so much. I am alone in my cell, and I'm having a hard time getting used to the loneliness. At least at Alexanderplatz I had the comfort of knowing that Zbyszek was not far away,[10] and I also miss the sweet and cheerful cell mate I used to have. Apart from that, life here has its good side. My cell is large and warm. They've taught me how to sew on a pedal machine, which is in my room, and I work from breakfast until supper. In the evening I can read since we have lights until eight, and we get two books a week. Before dinner, we have a little free time, and we can go for a walk in the

---

10. Zbyszek, her fiancé, was also a prisoner at Alexanderplatz at the time.

courtyard. We also have a chapel in the prison, and I can attend Mass on Sunday. And the food is better here than at Alexanderplatz.

Don't worry about my health. I am well. Really, things couldn't be better than here. After all, I can write you a long letter every two weeks and tell you everything. Please give my best to Karol,[11] and tell him that I never realized what a wonderful friend he was. It's so good of him to visit you from time to time. Please show him this letter, which I wrote [in German] without any help, and ask him if he's pleased with his student. I think I told you before that I've seen Zbyszek twice. You can imagine how thrilled we were to meet; what a day that was! Give Pani Wanda my best and reassure her, tell her that Zbyszek will most certainly return to her.

In front of my window there are two trees, and I can see a bit of sky. In the corner of my cell there lives a little spider—he is my only companion.

Dearest Mummy, this letter would never end if I were to write all the thoughts that go through my head—this solitude will soon turn me into a philosopher.

You know something, dear Mummy, sometimes I think that life makes no sense, I am not so attached to life as I used to be. I have only one wish, and that is to cheer you up, to make you happier than you are at present. Please Mummy, be brave, hold your head high!

Tell Father that I got his letter from Brwinów, and it made me very happy. Give my best regards to the Mierkowskis and to all my friends. Kisses to you and Father.

Your Tina

---

11. Karol Szapiro, a young Jew from Łódź, was living in Warsaw, with his parents under an assumed name using forged Latvian passports. Krystyna first met him when her family and the Szapiros took shelter in a church after they were forced out of their homes by the German army. Krystyna and Karol later met again in Warsaw and fell in love.

Alt-Moabit, Berlin
February 28, 1943

My most beloved parents,

I've been happy all day knowing that today I would be permitted to write you a letter. These few letters are, after all, the one slender thread joining us together.

I don't know how to thank you for the parcels and letters, which I received a couple of days ago. I received all the parcels addressed to Alexanderplatz. Only the one containing the pillow got lost. Dear parents, your packages give me such pleasure. How thrilled I was by the lovely dried flowers from the Polish meadow. The picture you sent me, Mummy, I've hung over my bed. Thank you for the navy blue skirt, comb, and shampoo. Yesterday I washed my hair, and today it is gloriously soft and shiny. Please send me more postage stamps and shampoo, otherwise I need nothing at the moment.

Dear Father, your letter made me so happy, but yet it also made me cry a little. You know, when I read such loving words, I suddenly realize what I have lost. Unfortunately, the time has passed when you could shelter me in your arms from life's terrors; I am a grown woman now and must look after myself. But I will always be brave—that I promise you—and I shall never lose hope. Never lose hope—that is my motto. I also received a card from Janek. Tell him I am very grateful. The poor idealist thinks that a new age will dawn when people will be better and there will be no more war. I'm afraid I don't believe that.

I'm still alone in my cell sewing blouses all day. My one comfort is that I get beautiful books to read. Last week I got a book about Switzerland; I felt I was breathing the cool fresh air of the Alps. Now I'm reading *Théâtre de Corneille* in French. Often I think about the past—what are my friends doing—Lolek and others? Will I see them soon? When I take my walk in the yard during my free hour, I look up at the sky, and I smile with joy when I see the clouds floating high above the prison walls. I feel sorry for people who are surrounded every day by even more beautiful sights, but can't find joy in them because their hearts are constricted and cold.

7

Pray for me, my beloved Mummy, maybe my fate will soon be settled.

Dear Father, forward this letter immediately to Warsaw.[12] Do this for me because Mummy might be worried again. I send my best regards to all my friends and I kiss and hug you with all my heart. Please, write to me often.

Your Tina

Alt-Moabit, Berlin
March 14, 1943

Dearest parents,

Thank you for your letters and parcels. I got two packages from Father and three from Mummy—with shampoo, toothpaste, postage stamps, and a pretty postcard. Mummy, please send me some "Camellia" sanitary napkins, a little mirror, my old blue silk blouse, and buy me some blue—navy blue—sandals, but make sure they're not too ugly!

Dear, kind Mummy, I feel less lonely now that I get so many loving letters from you; if only I could enclose my heart with this letter and cheer you a little. I would love to tell you more about my situation, but I am afraid to because everything was secret. You knew nothing about what I was doing because I told you nothing. Nor do you know about military law. It seems to be very severe. I am now in a military [war] court. If it is possible, perhaps you should get me a private lawyer, but this must be arranged quite quickly, if one indeed could help me. I didn't want to tell you about this before so as not to worry you, but the matter is now quite serious.

When I get a letter, I want to laugh and to cry. At first I feel so close to you, and then I feel myself painfully abandoned. But letters are really

---

12. Krystyna had to write in German because of the prison censor. These letters went first to her father who translated them before forwarding them to her mother.

the only comfort and joy. At Alexanderplatz, my friend and I were so in tune. We never cried together: if one was depressed and cried, the other comforted her.

This week, I was put to work packing medicines, pleasant and light work. Spring arrives earlier here than at home. The spring shrubs are big, budding. I saw them when I was washing windows.

Dear Father, you must tell me how your work in the garden is coming along. The weather here is splendid, making this prison desert harder for me to bear.

Don't worry about my health, Mummy. That is not, at the moment, so very important. When Pani Wanda writes to Zbyszek, tell her to send him my love. I am sure that he is sad that we are separated again. He is still so in love with me. I am glad that your money worries are over, dear Mummy, and that things are going better for Janek. At night, in my bed, I compose endless, long letters to you in my mind—far too long for the sheet of paper I get. You can't possibly imagine how much I love you.

I kiss you with all my heart, and send my love to all my friends, especially Alina,[13] Karol, and Zbyszek's family.

Your Tina

How delighted I was to recognize your handwriting, dear, kind friend![14] You are for me someone from another world, someone who will soon forget about me. What am I to you, Karol? A thought, a memory? But in your world there is no time for reflection and memories. I, on the other hand, am lost in the past and like a stern judge, I examine my life. Here, in prison, one can recognize the important things in life. In freedom, one can get lost in daily cares and all kinds of details. Here we acquire some distance, and so we see life as a whole. Life can only be understood if one believes in God, but even then one often asks—why? Sometimes I find it so hard. You know so well how spoiled I was, how

---

13. Her aunt, only slightly older than Krystyna, with whom she stayed and worked in Warsaw. Alina's husband, Stanislaw Gołębiowski, was killed in battle on September 5, 1939.

14. Note to her beloved Karol Szapiro, enclosed with the letter to her parents.

much love and understanding I demanded from everybody. Now I tell myself: Can't you finally teach yourself to settle everything with God by yourself? Do you have to always have someone who will comfort and cheer you? You must learn to be independent!

Alt-Moabit, Berlin
March 28, 1943

Beloved parents,

First I must thank you for your letters and parcels. Everything is delivered intact and complete, dear Mummy, don't worry about that. The parcels are opened in my presence by the *Anstaltmutter*,[15] who is good to us and deserves this name.

Your packages, Mummy, are splendid and very good for the teeth. However, don't send them more than once a week. I loved the rose garland, the picture, and the pretty postcards. I see that you want to keep on spoiling me, my dearest Mummy, whom I love with all my heart! And from you, Father, I always get precisely what I need most.

I am healthy, serene, and working at the present time doing finishing work by hand on light, brightly colored dresses. We have splendid spring weather here. Only now do I understand what it means to long for one's lost country. I have everything I need here, but even a golden cage is hard on a bird accustomed to freedom. I sit and sew. Before my eyes are images of familiar places. I hear the sound of birds singing. I feel the light touch of a fresh breeze. Ahh, if only I could be there again. I can see long-forgotten faces with amazing clarity; I hear their voices. My childhood and my youth are passing before my eyes like a film. I never think about the future. But I don't want to be sad, and although I

---

15. Literally "institution mother," the first reference to Hedwig Grimpe, the guard later called Sonnenschein (ray of sunshine).

don't have a good voice, I sing all the songs I know. That helps. I pray all the time, arms outstretched, but I sometimes feel it's all for nothing. I try to think of all kinds of ways, my most beloved Mummy, how I could help you. You know, when I am sad, I tell myself that I am not alone in my sadness, that there are many people who suffer more. Think of those mothers who have lost more than one child in the war, and instead of being one who is always lost in worry, try at least once to be one who gives comfort to others. That will make you feel so good—you'll see! I received 50 RM [Reichmarks] from Widzew.[16] I didn't really need them, but since I have them, I will subscribe to a newspaper if they let me. My progress in German I owe above all to my friend [Mimi] at the Alex [Alexanderplatz]. She was a splendid, clever young woman.

Dear Pani Wanda. I was so pleased to get your letter. I love you very much and share your anxiety about your son. Sometimes I feel I love him like a mother. These hard trials did not weaken him, quite the contrary. He is stronger, and he has great faith. I'm sure his faith will always help him. I am convinced that his fate will be easier than mine. Please give my best to all the dear aunts and thank them for all the wonderful days I spent in Podków.

It was wonderful to hear from Alina. They were the first Polish words to reach me here. Have you written anything new, Alina? I am thinking now of your poem about spring. We used to say back then that we dreaded a boring life! Kiss your sweet children for me. I think all these things that are happening, all this human suffering, must serve some higher purpose, which we, with our human limitations, cannot understand.

Beloved parents, I think it best if you don't make any great plans for my future. Better a pleasant surprise than a bitter disappointment. Mummy, please send me my blue jersey blouse, the one that doesn't need ironing.

Heartfelt hugs and kisses.

Your Tina

---

16. A town in Poland. Sender unknown.

Alt-Moabit, Berlin
April 11, 1943

Beloved parents,

I thank you with all my heart for your letters and parcels; they are my one great joy here and a great boost for my morale. I am very grateful for your efforts to get me a lawyer; I hope that he will be able to see me soon.

I was so thrilled, my dear Mummy, to get a card from you written in Polish. What a feast! The clogs are perfect; don't worry, Mummy, everything you sent was delivered to me, including the postage stamps. I am in good health. A couple of weeks ago I told the prison doctor that I once suffered from lung disease, so he sent me to the hospital for X-rays. I haven't been informed of the results, but if you wish, I can ask about them.

As for my sentence, I know what it will be. I have not been in an interrogation prison for the past six months for nothing, and the Gestapo officers couldn't wait to tell me what I should expect. It's not so bad. With time, one can learn to live with any thought. What torments me most are memories of my childhood and youth, and these thoughts stay with me far into the night. I enjoy a brief respite when, between my last meal and nightfall, I immerse myself in reading, and I am overjoyed when, on Mondays, I once again get two fat books. Thanks to the money you sent me, Mummy, I get a newspaper every day. It's the *Berliner Lokal-Anzeiger*. Now I will know everything that is going on in the world. Now I must tell you a secret. I made myself a little doll out of spools of thread, and I play with her. I call her Mimi—after my good friend from the Alex. No matter what you do, you need somebody. Solitude teaches one a lot, but it has its limitations. The prophets had to go into the desert in order to hear God, but they could only take this solitude for forty days.

Sundays are the most boring days here. There's no mail, no work. On the other hand, nobody bothers me, and, alone in my cell, I could stand on my head if that's what I wanted to do. You know what is the most frustrating? When you're alone, you can cry, but you can't laugh. For that, you absolutely need company! I once tried to laugh all by myself, but I quickly had the unpleasant sensation that I was losing my sanity.

No doubt you will spend Easter with Janek in Borowin, and all the good aunts will be shaking their heads, carrying on about Zbyszek and me. Well, I wish you all a Happy Easter! I want Janek to say "Hello" to the forest for me when he goes for a walk. I miss forests and meadows more than I miss people, with the exception, of course, of you, dearest parents, and all my dearest friends. The happiest times of my life are associated with the beauty of nature. That is God's greatest gift to mankind, the gift of which I am now deprived. I recently got a postcard from Janek. I can see that he is overcome with love for his little son. A very happy father.

My most beloved Mummy, you must not say that I am your one joy; you still have Halinka and Kola. I love you so much, Mummy; as the war continued, I always admired your courage and daring. You know, the first night after my arrest, lying not in my soft, comfortable bed but on the hard pallet in a horrible cell, I thought only of you, how will you bear this unbearable event. And later, when they were transporting me to Szucha,[17] and I saw the crowds of people on the street, happy people who glanced with such indifference at the van, I realized then that I was no longer one of them. After dark, when I can no longer read, I sit on the side of my cot, but I am not really here. I am with you, in Warsaw, in Brwinów; I can see you so clearly.

I used to hallucinate at first, much as you did, Mummy, but in time this stopped. Could you do something special for Zbyszek? He is such a pathetic child. He worried, much as I do, that you are angry with him. Don't send me any illustrated magazines; they are forbidden. But do write more about the Mierkowskis. Are they always so good to you? What is Januszek doing?[18]

I wish you a very happy Easter and kiss you all. Give my best wishes and hugs to all my friends, especially Alina and Karol.

Your Tina

---

17. The Gestapo interrogation center in Warsaw.
18. The Mierkowskis' son.

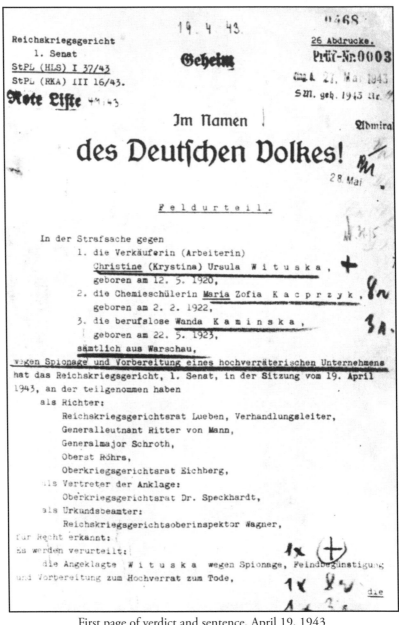

First page of verdict and sentence, April 19, 1943

There is no problem here getting permission for visits. Unfortunately you are a little too far away, and in Berlin I have neither friends nor relatives.

Dear Pani Wanda, the Pascal Lamb[19] is so sweet. I'm at a loss for words to tell you how much pleasure it gave me. I wish I could express my gratitude and love for you in some tangible way.

Alt-Moabit, Berlin
April 25, 1943

Beloved parents,

No doubt by now you have been informed by our defense counsel that on April 19, I was sentenced to death for spying and for treason. I did not lose my courage; I maintained my dignity. For many long months I prepared myself for the possibility that I will have to die. My heart only aches for you, knowing how you must be suffering.

But you shouldn't lose all hope. I spoke two days ago with my lawyer, who reassured me that there may be some way out of my situation, and there still remains the possibility of clemency. And there are still about three months left before the sentence is executed, so I have time to write more than one long letter to you.

I will ask for permission to send you all the things that I will no longer need. I am so glad that the other two girls got lighter sentences. I love them both like sisters. People on the outside imagine that someone sentenced to death must go mad from fear and anguish. In fact, it's quite the contrary. Maybe that's because it's beyond comprehension. I couldn't sleep the first night, and I cried a bit, but only because of you,

---

19. Pascal Lamb, an Easter religious symbol, probably an illustration on a card.

my best and most beloved Mummy. I didn't even consider suicide. I will not take on myself the responsibility for my death.

I am not alone right now and that is wonderful. With me is a Polish woman from Warsaw who was on the same train with me to Berlin, was at the Alex the whole time I was there, and now is sharing my sad fate with me. She is my age, a good, dignified young woman. We talk all day long, we have so much to tell one another, all the things we experienced and felt while we were in solitary. We discovered that we have mutual friends in Poland; our country is so small that everybody knows everybody else. Today is Easter, the day of the Resurrection, and on this day I must write about such sad things.

We now have permission to go to church, and this morning we sang in the chapel: "Gone now are the terrors of the grave. Death, where now is your victory?" I want to believe that someday we shall all be together again, that I won't be alone there where I will go. So many of my young friends will be with me: Lolo, Staś, Tomek, Zbyszek. Death is the salvation of all people, and in this life I believe only in this one great truth that one sees so often etched on prison walls: "And this too shall pass." I am not afraid of death, at least no more than I would be before some serious operation; it takes, after all, just a moment—and then it's all over.

You must be brave, my best Mummy, chin up and forgive me for putting you through this. Maybe . . . maybe, it will still turn out all right. There is always plenty of time for sadness.

I am also worried about Zbyszek. Better not write to him yet about what happened. He is sad enough right now. I am sure he will not grieve too long; I was for him, at most, a beautiful dream. When we were at the Alex, I prepared him for the worst, and he promised me that he would not be silly.

I received your huge parcel, and I was so happy that I almost forgot about my death sentence; I haven't seen so many good things all at once in a long time. I look pretty much as before, but I don't have much of an appetite right now and have a hard time eating what they give me.

Spring is magnificent here. The lilacs are in bloom, as are the magnolias and the chestnut trees. I finally got to see a bit of Berlin on my way to the military court. We drove past the Zoological Gardens. When you see everything bursting with life, it's impossible to think about death.

Mummy, I no longer need money, of course; just send me my navy silk dress and some shampoo. I will always be vain, and I will curl my hair even on the last day. They took away my little doll. Pity, because I wanted to send her to you as a memento. We are not allowed to play here; we must only work and atone for our sins. I could, of course, still appeal for clemency; in that case maybe Daddy could remind them that back in the days when he was in Warsaw, he once saved the lives of a German family.

Once again I beg of you. Hold your heads high and write often. I think of you all the time and send kisses from the bottom of my heart. I didn't get the medicines you sent, such things are forbidden.

Dear Karol. So our friendship is coming to an end. I wanted so much to know how your life would unfold. You know, on the wall of my cell at the Alex, someone wrote in big letters: "Everything because of your great love." So I realized that I was not really alone.

Your Tina

Sweet, beloved Mummy, don't cry so much!

Alt-Moabit, Berlin
May 9, 1943

Beloved parents,

I hope that the censors will not have anything against these last few letters being written in Polish. I would like you to understand them too, my dearest Mummy. I've received your wonderful, heartfelt letters. Naturally, on such an occasion I had to cry a little because I feel so terribly sorry for you and feel so guilty because I've never brought you much joy, only worries. I breathed a sigh of relief that you are not in despair and have not given up hope.

Thank you for all your words of encouragement and reassurance, for thinking of me. I feel very well, and I am so cheerful that I feel guilty. Here I am perfectly happy while there you are all worried and thinking heavens know what. We are now three and we all have the same concerns. Olga [Jędrkiewicz] is from Warsaw and is my age, while Monika [Dymska], from Toruń, is twenty-five.[20] Olga is very beautiful and both are awfully nice. You can't imagine how wonderful it is, after a few months of solitary confinement, to once again have young friends and be able to talk as much as we like. I hardly ever think about what awaits me because I simply don't have time for that. All day long we sing, joke, and behave very much like playful girls at boarding school. We feel like we are in boarding school because there are so many things forbidden here, and we're afraid we will get a scolding. All three of us have a sewing machine: Monika for making buttonholes, I for hem-stitching, while Olga sews very pretty dresses. At night we have to put the machines out into the corridor so we have enough room for sleeping. I sleep on the bed, and they on mattresses on the floor, but they are not at all upset by that because the bed is just as hard as the floor. In any case, we sleep very well. It's the month of May, so every evening we sing hymns to our Blessed Mother and in the daytime all the folksongs, army songs, and popular songs that we know. You know, Alina,[21] it is as cheerful here as it used to be in the shop.

Beloved parents, I have one final, difficult duty ahead of me, to remain brave and dignified until the end. Pray for me, dearest Mummy, that in the event that I do not get clemency, and one beautiful day they take me away to the place where I will die, pray that I can do this. I didn't write my appeal until today because the lawyer said he would come to help me, but he didn't get here until now. Thank you from the bottom of my heart for all your efforts. I pray every day for God to save me, not just for myself but for you. The act of beheading lasts one second, and then I will be free of all fear and worries, but you will never be able to forget my death.

About your visit here, dearest little Mummy, I wrote a *Wunschzettel*

---

20. Olenka [Olga] Jędrkiewicz and Monika Dymska, Krystyna's cell mates in cell #18.

21. Her young aunt.

[a list of requests] to the military court. But think about this carefully. A ten-minute visit may cause you even greater heartache. Would you not return to Warsaw even more brokenhearted? At least now, you have grown accustomed to my not being near you.

My best loved Daddy. Your brief letter revealed to me how much you think about me and how terribly worried you are about the latest news. I know that you didn't entirely realize how serious my situation was, and it tore me apart whenever I had to write to you about it. I was thrilled to get all your parcels. The little bunny you sent me, Mummy, is so exquisite that I can't get enough of him and carry him about all day in the pocket of my apron. Thank you also for the pendant of good-luck charms, which I divided immediately and shared with my friends.

Thank dear Pani Wanda and all the good aunts for their tender letter from Borowin. I truly believe that with so many good souls caring for me, nothing bad can happen to me. Do you agree now that I was right in wanting to see a lot and do a lot? Maybe I had a premonition that I didn't have much time left. Halinka finally sent me a photograph of little Kola. What a splendid, sweet little baby. I'm thrilled with him. Both photos are now on our little table. Olga made frames for them. I think that now that she has her little son, Halinka doesn't want to know about anything else in the world. She writes to me as though I were on holidays at the seashore rather than in prison. I suppose they have already sent you my watch and gold chain with the two pendants. Put the little dog [a charm] in a safe place, Mummy. I got it from a very dear person who is probably no longer alive.[22] I was to deliver it to his mother but I may never get back to Poland. Today I am terribly happy because my beloved friend [Mimi Terwiel], who was with me in the last jail, is here again. Actually, we can't be in the same cell as before, but we see one another every day during *Freistund* [free time], and we can smile at one another. What a shame that you can never get to meet her, my beloved parents, because she is truly a magnificent woman.

---

22. A present from Janek, a fellow prisoner who was in an adjacent cell at the Alex. He fell in love with Krystyna's voice. Originally from Suwałk, he was wounded in the leg during his escape from Auschwitz. He expected a death sentence and disappeared one day without a trace.

I finally got permission to send home the things I no longer need, however, they said that if I decide to do that, I must send everything except what I am wearing. Therefore I decided to wait a while, until I am notified whether my verdict will be upheld, or reprieved.

Our prison days are much longer now because it is light until nine o'clock—and we say "good night" to one another at ten. I get up at six, and as soon as I am out of bed, I exercise a bit. Olga, the pessimist, sometimes insists that there's no point in it, but I have decided to continue as always even until the last day. Then we wash from head to toe with cold water, and we argue, jokingly, about who gets the wash basin first. We fold our bed linen and wipe the floor with a wet cloth. Then I prepare everything for breakfast because I hold the position of mistress of the house, but they have to wash up after, something I've never liked doing. In the meantime, Olga and I plot all manner of mischief, which ends in such uproarious laughter that our cell is really considered the most cheerful one here.

My beloved parents, I often wish you could get a glimpse of me, at least for a moment; I am sure that would ease some of the pain in your hearts. It is pleasant now during *Freistund* because it's warm, and the four trees in the courtyard are in full leaf. Forget-me-nots, lily of the valley, and other wonderful things are in full bloom in the flowerbeds. If you come to visit me, Mummy, then you will see this courtyard where I walk every day, head held high. Every two weeks we get clean towels, dishcloths, and shirts. We look very funny in these shirts because they are very thick, long, and so wide that I could get two of me in them. I seem lost inside, which makes Olga once again roar with laughter. That's when I think of that lovely silk lingerie Daddy gave me. What ironic fate! Now I am always wearing the navy skirt and blue jersey blouse; it is quite cool in our cell because the walls are incredibly thick, and the sun peeps in only for an hour in the morning. It is dry here compared to the Alex, where it was so damp you could get stuck to the walls, and hygienic conditions in general are first-rate. There are very nice bathrooms here with bathtubs where we bathe every two weeks.

Chin up, dearest Mummy, and don't worry about me. My peerless father—it's not for nothing that I am your daughter; I can bear the ups and downs of life very bravely.

I kiss you a thousand times and all those whom I love. Little brother-in-law, Janusz, thank you for your note.

[Note in the margin] Oh, my dearest, sweetest Karol, do you know what? I am writing with the pen that you gave me for my Name Day.[23] I also used it to write my *Gnadengesuch* [appeal].

[unsigned]

Alt-Moabit, Berlin
May 23, 1943

Beloved parents,

I am so pleased that you have not given up hope; your letters bring me such joy! The past few days I have been extremely happy because I realized that you, dearest Mummy, are apparently the bravest of all mothers; that was the best news I could have got. I am really very proud of you. I worry that something terrible might happen to you; I received your card in which you write about the bombing of Warsaw. So long as I know that you are all right, I feel fine. We three are all getting along splendidly, and we are in good health except for poor Monika, who frequently breaks out in cold sores. Not surprisingly, we are a little pale, since we never get to see the sun, and we must look like weeds that sprouted in a dark cellar. I am so pleased that you met Olenka's mother. We are extremely fond of one another; we understand each other and so can be very straightforward with one another, more so than with Monika, who, though she is a terrific optimist, is not so cheerful as Olenka and I. Marysia and Wanda[24] are heartwarming, aren't they? Both have such strong characters and hearts of gold. Never in my life have I ever had so many friends.

---

23. Celebrated like a birthday.
24. Marysia Kacprzyk and Wanda Kamińska, arrested with Krystyna.

Thank you so much for my birthday presents; naturally I was delighted. My last birthday, despite everything, was quite pleasant; I got lots of good wishes and some presents. Olenka gave me an elephant made of coat material, a cardboard box for my letters, a bookmark, and a piece of bread. That piece of bread was the most touching because that dear person who gave it to me has a pretty good appetite herself. Olenka and Monika sang *Sto lat* [a song wishing one a "hundred years"]—a bit of black humor under the circumstances, I must say. We also often have all kinds of "headless dreams." All day long we sew diligently; the cell is filled with the sounds of sewing machines and our singing; we are up to our necks in brightly colored blouses and flowered dresses. We call ourselves "Salon de mode K.O.M." [Krystyna, Olenka, Monika].

We sing a lot; a favorite is that sad song about the little eagles of Lvov whose refrain goes: "With a bleeding wound on my breast, I leave you; only for you, Mummy, only for Poland, do I grieve." Last Sunday we all went to confession and received Holy Communion. I was very upset with the news about Miodek.[25] You have not written for a long time about Zbyszek, Mummy. When I was interrogated about him, the police officer assured me that I would be present at his trial, so I still hope that I will see him at least one more time. I would give anything for that. The best thing for him would be to remain as long as possible at the Alex. I hope with all my heart that he will. Is Pani Wanda taking it well? And is Dudek[26] still in Podków?

Dear Alina, I think of you often and share your great anxiety. Please, don't give up hope. Surely it's impossible that God would not hear your prayers. I long for the day when these dark times are behind you and your life is filled with sunshine again.

Dear Mummy, tell me, did Bruno[27] write to me after my arrest? Does he know what happened to me? We did as you suggested with the sugar, Mummy, and Olenka and I came to the conclusion that our mothers are most creative. The washing powder, glycerin, and shampoo are so much appreciated. We share the little pillow, each of us taking

---

25. A young friend of Krystyna.
26. Zbyszek's brother.
27. Relationship unknown.

turns sleeping on it, and sometimes we toss it around and catch it like a ball. There's one thing I want to ask you. Write to me often and enclose one clean sheet of paper each time. Please send me my navy dress with the little flowers on it; it is most suitable for prison life. Also, please send a package of "Camellia" and a notebook and pencil. They might permit me that.

I received your package yesterday, Daddy, but I've been waiting impatiently for your letter for several days. I was so sorry I did not write to Halina in time for her birthday; I didn't think of it early enough. I am shocked by the news of the death of my dearest friend's fiancé [Helmut Himpel].[28] What torments me most is my helplessness; I can't go to her and comfort her. To be separated by only a few meters and not be able to speak to one another—that is so terrible. Please, Mummy, pray for her always, as you pray for me. You must write about Olenka's mother—how does she look, how does she feel? I wish I had your photographs. You know what, Mummy, ask Maryna's brother to take a picture of you; he's a marvelous photographer. And you must write to me more about your life; I find it hard to picture you because I don't know what you do all day. What's new in Brwinów? Are there guests? Karol, why aren't you writing to me? You probably don't know how to comfort me, what to say to me, but that is not at all important. As for my fate, I find myself right now in a state of complete detachment, a state I hope to maintain until the end. One's own death is not half so terrible as is the death of someone you love, and that is why I feel so unbearably sad when I think of you, my beloved parents. Olenka looks quite good, though pale, and sometimes she is so lovely one can hardly take one's eyes off her. Dearest Daddy, you must write to me because I miss you so much. I wanted to finish this letter on a humorous note, but I got so upset about this terrible news [Helmut's execution] that my sense of humor abandoned me and I have used three handkerchiefs.

Hugs and kisses to Pani Wanda, all the dear aunts, Alina, Karol, and Mr. and Mrs. Mierkowski, Janusz, and Leszek, and you, dearest parents, I kiss most of all.

Your Tina

---

28. Mimi's fiancé, Helmut Himpel, arrested with Mimi and executed.

Alt-Moabit, Berlin
May 30, 1943

Beloved parents,

I wonder, did you get my letter of last week and the card for Daddy? I haven't heard from Daddy for a long time, which worries me, but I hope to hear something any day. Yesterday I got your parcel, Mummy, with the scarves and a necklace. I thank you so much; it means so much to me that you think of all these things, but we aren't allowed to wear any ornaments here. Please don't send any more food parcels either, but do send me the navy dress with the flowers.

I was so terribly upset with the news about Karol, I simply burst into tears when I got your card. My poor, sweet Karol, what could have happened to him?[29] Now that I know what it means to suffer, to be lonely, I would like to protect everyone from these things, and I always pray that God will look after all my loved ones at home. I am terribly worried about you. We hear all kinds of things here about Warsaw. It is sad that you won't have darling Karol to cheer you anymore, but maybe he'll still turn up! I would so grieve for him, how sad that all those from whom we could expect so much in the future are dying. Please let me know immediately if you hear something about him. In the meantime, try to comfort Mrs. Szapiro and kiss her for me.

Did Zbyszek not write to his mother? I only know that he has been moved. How is Pani Wanda? Is she in good health? I am so grateful to her that she thinks of you; if only I could repay all the debts I am accumulating. Do you know what is the most painful thing about our lives here? That we know of so many human tragedies, and we can't help anyone nor even comfort anyone. We are completely powerless within these four walls, yet we feel everything. Perhaps my letter will seem very sad to you. Don't get upset, dearest Mummy—this is just momentary bitterness, and then we, Olenka and I, will once again begin to sing and joke.

---

29. Karol disappeared and, at this point, is probably in hiding. Details are not known.

All three of us are well, only I don't look so good because I have been sick and in some pain, but I've been to the prison infirmary, got medication, and am recovering. Monika and Olenka are indulging me terribly because of this and won't let me lift so much as a stool for fear I might tire myself. I have here in my cell your photograph, Mummy—we framed it and it's standing on our little table—now I no longer envy Olenka, who has long had a photo of her mother and sister and kisses it daily. Halinka doesn't put herself out; in all these months she wrote me only one letter and a card. Remind her, Mummy, to hurry because if she doesn't think of it soon, it may be too late.

You must write to me about the bombing in Warsaw, which streets suffered most and whether any of our friends were killed; I am so interested in what is happening to you all and what your spirits are like; if only I could be there just for one hour!

I must tell you what we can see through our window: a bit of garden surrounded by a high wall, behind which is an acacia, a maple, a wild lilac, and a tree we can't identify, and about which we've had many arguments. One part of the garden is cultivated with a few rather miserable, prison-like flowers and sixteen tomato plants (I counted them). The acacia was blooming, and its scent would have reached us were it not for the smell of some rabbit cages, which must be somewhere nearby. That smell brought back some childhood memories. A titmouse has a nest in the acacia, and we dread the thought that the prison cat, a big white cat that makes a mess in the garden, will eat her. There's another cat here, a black one that we don't see much of, but that, Olenka claims, brings us bad luck. But in fact, our window is quite high, and the bottom half of the pane is frosted, so we don't look out very often. I've been refused permission to have you visit, so if you really want to, you must try to get permission from your side.

Dearest Mummy, send me a thick notebook and a pencil, which I am now allowed to have, and also another mirror because I gave mine to my friend, my dearest one, for whom I asked you to pray whenever you pray for me. Daddy, maybe tomorrow I will get a letter from you; in the meantime, I know from Mummy that I am in your thoughts. I kiss you both. Best regards to Alina, Pani Wanda, all the dear aunts, and Mr. and Mrs. Mierkowski.

Your Tina

Kisses to Olenka's mother.

Dear and cherished second Mother.[30] Please forgive me for addressing you this way, but in the month I've been with Krysia [Krystyna], I've come to know her so well and love her like a sister, and she has told me so much about you.

Krysia is so brave and is not at all worried about her situation, believing, as we all do, that she will get clemency. She is in perfect health, and if sometimes she doesn't look too good, it is only because of prison conditions. She is always cheerful and smiling. Thank you for remembering me in dedicating a Holy Mass to us. With best wishes, Ola J.

Alt-Moabit, Berlin
June 6, 1943

Beloved parents,

I wonder if you got my letter of May 23. I enclosed it with Olenka's letter to her mother, but we just discovered, much to our sorrow, it was stopped by the censor because Olenka wrote about her trial, and that is forbidden. Did Daddy get my card? I am worried because you don't write to me at all, dearest Daddy. Every day I wait for a letter from you.

Here time flies at a frightening pace when one thinks that each day brings us closer to the moment when the question of our life or our death will be decided. It would please me to know as quickly as possible; I want all this behind me. We are getting on very well, and we

---

30. Note in the margin written by Olenka Jędrkiewicz to Krystyna's mother.

don't lose our good humor; each day is so much like another that we can't really keep track of time, and I was amazed today when I realized that it's been two months since my trial. Don't worry about me, dearest Mummy, my companions are all in good health, and I too am perfectly well. Thank you very much for the parcels, but don't send me any more food.[31] We just have to get along without this, and, in fact, it would ease our consciences if you didn't spend so much money on us. In previous letters, I asked you, Mummy, to send me my navy print dress, "Camellia," a notebook, and a pencil. Your last package with the candy got here already. I don't understand why you haven't yet received my watch and chain. I was specifically called to the office in connection with this matter, and I gave them your address. We are not permitted any luxuries or watches in prison, so these things are kept in security. I really don't need any money, Mummy. I don't understand why you don't want me to send my things, after all, why should they remain here if they could be of use in Warsaw, if not for you or Halina, then for so many other needy people. You needn't worry that you will have to go to the Gestapo about this, they will simply send it to you by post.

My God, to think that I too created only problems for you and never gave you any comfort.

I came to love little Mimi, my cell mate at the Alex, so much that now I know what it means to be completely powerless to help one's loved one, to not be able to go to her and comfort her, when I know that she is unhappy and alone.

Karol's fate fills me with anxiety. Write to me immediately as soon as you hear something about him. I've received your card telling me that Zbyszek is now here at Moabit. Actually, I had hoped he would be able to stay at the Alex as long as possible, but of course his case can't go on forever. I expect that I will see him at his trial; we certainly won't be allowed to meet before then. I wrote him a note and sent it off with the hope that it would get to him. I trust that you complied with my request and didn't inform him of my sentence. I wouldn't want him to know about it before his trial. I am confident that everything will turn

---

31. Most food packages were confiscated.

out better for him than it did for me, that at least he will some day return and comfort you, my beloved Mummy.

Dear Halinka. Yesterday I got your letter in which you write about your happy family and how well you are managing. It amazes us here, so cut off from normal life, that there are places on this earth where life goes on so smoothly, happily as before. To us it seems that the whole world must be engulfed in the flames of war, that everywhere people are fighting and killing or weeping and in agony. Lucky Halinka, may your family's nest, sheltered in a distant village, escape this unhappy fate. It seems to me that I was never intended for such a serene life; I was always drawn to extremes, and this continues even here. No doubt you will be surprised if I tell you that I would like to live so I could continue studying, and I regret terribly the time that I have wasted. Dear Olenka and I often talk far into the night, after the ever-sleepy Monika has fallen asleep, about every possible subject, and we have come to the conclusion that if we were ever able to return to normal life, our outlook on life and the world would be very different from that of other people. We feel as though we are standing on a ship's plank over the deep ocean, and it's amazing that in this position, instead of getting dizzy, it's quite the opposite—we are clearheaded and can evaluate everything and everybody objectively. We are no longer part of a crowd whose spirit could influence our feelings or our judgment.

Lots of kisses to you, Halinka, and to Jan and the little one. And you, beloved parents, I kiss most of all and think of you always. Best regards to all those whom I love.

Your Tina

Please send me a little mirror, Mummy, because I gave mine to Mimi, and please pray for me.

Alt-Moabit, Berlin
June 13, 1943

Dear parents,

The 11th of June was the happiest day since our imprisonment. Olenka's sentence was commuted. The Führer mercifully changed her death sentence to five years in a severe penal camp (*verschärfter Straflager*). We were delirious with joy, all three of us because we love one another so much, and I perhaps most of all because I have become very attached to Olenka. Now if I were reassured about my little Mimi, I would be the happiest person in Moabit. On Friday morning Olenka was summoned by the supervisor. Monika and I were terror stricken because we assumed this meant a confirmation of the [death] sentence. We were standing in the corridor waiting for our *Freistund,* when Olenka came down from upstairs, her little face beaming. The first day, Olenka couldn't believe her good fortune. It is hard to get accustomed to the idea of life when for three months you are preparing yourself for death. I am only sorry that we will have to part because now she won't remain here longer than a month. But that is prison life—you leave those whom you have come to love, suddenly, and sometimes without even time to say good-bye.

Today is Pentecost. We went this morning to the chapel; we got bread with margarine for breakfast. It is sunny outside. We don't have to work, so we are writing letters and reading books. Such is the holiday spirit. I imagine that crowds of people went today to Podków and Brwinów; those long-ago places sometimes seem so close, as though I saw them only yesterday.

Marysia and Wanda look well. Wanda will be leaving us at any moment because her sentence too has been confirmed.[32] It will be hard to say good-bye to her because she is our "golden heart." For me it is so sad because whenever someone leaves, I have to tell myself that I will probably never see her again. But our good spirits never leave us, especially

---

32. Wanda Kamińska was sentenced to three years at Witten-Annen, a penal camp. Marysia Kacprzyk got eight years in a camp, but the prosecutor was still demanding the death penalty.

now, because of Olenka's good fortune. If there is anything I want to complain about, it is you, dearest parents. Daddy, you never write, and Mummy, you only send cards. If you only knew how we wait for letters, how much we worry about you and about Warsaw. I am grateful for the parcels, but I have already told you in my last letter not to send me food. I only need soap, washing powder, and shampoo. I will write to you more often now because the court gave me permission to do so. I feel bad that I've never had any visits: Monika had a visit from her sister, and Olenka saw a friend. It's quite stuffy in our cell now because it's quite hot outside, and we can't open the window properly; though still, we are happy when the sun occasionally shines in. I wrote a note to Zbyszek.

Dearest parents, I too would like to bring you this great joy and write to you that my life has been spared. But I must be prepared for anything; that is where human strength lies, that even the worst will not break us. Our lawyer[33] quite rightly told us that hope is the source of bewilderment and confusion.

I kiss you with all my heart, and please be in good spirits, as I am, and write to me. Kisses to all my friends.

Your Tina

Alt-Moabit, Berlin
June 1943[34]

We should be pleased with the news of the ratification of your sentence, but I feel very sad that you will leave us, you, our ray of sunshine, our

---

33. Alban Rehm, a court-appointed lawyer. Mrs. Wituska had contacted Albrecht Eitner, a German lawyer then in Warsaw, to ask for help in finding a defense attorney in Berlin. Eitner offered assistance to families whose relatives had fallen into the hands of the Gestapo, but it was later discovered that he did this only to get information about the underground. At one time, he served as president of the Council for the Disposition of Jewish Property. He was executed by the Home Army on July 1, 1944.

34. A letter smuggled to her friend Wanda Kamińska.

little joy. I had hoped that you would go together with Marysia, and I was happy that you would be always together. Instead you are leaving alone for an unknown world, and your little heart will long for your friends.

I know that you do not need our advice or our instructions; just be yourself, and I am sure you will find new friends who will come to love you as much as we do. Don't give up hope that you will see me again, but death does not frighten me, and if I must die, I will die happy at least knowing that you two dearest girls have been saved.

At Zuchthous you will not be able to get news from home as you did here, but be brave, little Wanda, and don't worry needlessly. I am sure you will somehow hear about our fates.

Ask Marysia to send me again, before she goes, her beautiful poems, if she still has them, and pray occasionally for my poor inconsolable Rosemarie [Mimi], who cannot come to terms with the loss of her beloved Helmut. Thank you again, Wanda, for your dear little heart of gold and for the sweet letter that brightened my mother's spirit.

Farewell, I kiss you a million times and wish you all good things.

Your K.

Alt-Moabit, Berlin
June 20, 1943

Dearest parents,

In my last letters I scolded you so much for not writing, and then all of a sudden, the next week, I got three letters, two from Mummy and one from Daddy. Therefore I withdraw everything and apologize for my outburst. Your letters are such a tremendous joy to me; I am in a completely different frame of mind when I get news from you. I am the most fortunate of all three of us because I am the only one whose parents are free. Olenka is terribly worried about her mother. We try to cheer her as much as we can. I also got two parcels, one from Mummy with the dress, and one from Daddy.

I sent Daddy's parcel to a friend at the Alex because they are allowed food parcels, so nothing is wasted. Many thanks for the dress and other things; today I got all dressed up in it for chapel and looked very chic. Olenka made a lovely collar for it out of my pink slip. You have no idea how inventive we have become here; with a little patience, one can create wonders out of nothing. Olenka is a true artist when it comes to handicrafts and sewing. What really pleases me is that you are so full of faith and hope about my safe return home; I no longer worry in the slightest about my situation. Yesterday, after getting our letters from home, we celebrated and laughed so loudly that we got a scolding. Prisons resemble schools in many respects, very strict schools. I received the 50 RM, Mummy, but it bothers me because there is no need to send them. I can buy stamps here. I especially want to thank you for the notebook and pencil. If I had literary talents, I would immediately start work on a novel. It would be terribly interesting, sometimes tragic, but not without humor, which never leaves us.

Thank you, Mummy, for the news about Zbyszek. He is terribly amusing with all those plans of his for the future while we are both sitting in prison and still don't know how it will all end. Even if we were both to survive, who knows what we would do. People go through such a complete transformation in jail. Sometimes I think I am much more mature than Zbyszek, even though I laugh a lot and like to fool around like a boarding school student, while he is always serious. I sometimes feel that compared to him, I am terribly old, though here I am often asked whether I am still a minor, and when the three of us were on trial, they referred to us as *Madchenpensjonat* [boarding school girls].

I've been to the dentist, Mummy, though I didn't have a toothache, but I decided to go because of all your admonitions. Fortunately, except for one little cavity that is not yet worth drilling and filling, he found nothing. Poor Monika had to have two teeth pulled and then swelled up terribly, and she is still in pain. You see, Mummy, how healthy I am? I have now been eight months behind bars, and I have suffered nothing except a headache. My friends Marysia and Wanda don't look bad either; I saw them today in chapel. Your photograph, along with my other photos, were taken from me by the police when I was arrested. After the interrogation, all my papers were returned to me, and they are now in safekeeping along with my other things. I am delighted that you will send me more "Lux" soap. You have no idea how beautifully it washes one's hair, just as well as shampoo. Yesterday we all washed one another's hair, and today we look like goddesses. We came to the conclusion, Olga and I, that if you are vain, nothing will change you, not even a death sentence.

Please thank Leszek[35] for his kind and heartwarming letter. How nice of him to think of me. Give my best to Mr. and Mrs. Mierkowski and little Janusz.

I can't stop thinking about what could have happened to Karol, it's so long since there's been any news of him. It's not so difficult to find out whether someone is at Pawiak or not.[36] And I wonder what has happened to Bruno. Perhaps he's still fighting, or maybe he has long since been killed at the front. If you should hear from him, do tell him that I haven't forgotten him. How strange life is! Give my best to Aunt Wanda and Aunt Stasia especially, and all the aunts, including Mrs. Dina Korsak. They are all so lovable that I get emotional just thinking about them, and I do long to see them all. Give my best regards to Mrs. Klonoska[37] and tell her that I am very touched that they remember me in their prayers. I wish them all good things. You must let me know whether my hairdresser's place has been bombed or not because he is on my list as one of the first I will visit when I get back to Warsaw, though I will never again dye my hair.

Dearest Mummy. I thank you from the bottom of my heart for all your efforts on my behalf, and when I get home, I will kiss you a million times. I will write Daddy a special card this week to thank him for his wonderful letter. We have an awful lot of work to do, but otherwise we keep busy reading French and German books.

Kisses to the two Janeks and to Kola. I'd give anything for a cigarette, but that is an impossible dream.

Hugs and kisses.

Your Tina

---

35. Relationship unknown.
36. The main Gestapo prison in Warsaw.
37. Relationship unknown.

Alt-Moabit, Berlin
June 27, 1943

Beloved parents,

I have just received Mummy's card telling me that Daddy is coming to Berlin. I really can't believe that I will be allowed to see him, and I try not to think about it because I couldn't bear the disappointment. In fact, I can't even imagine it—someone from home suddenly appearing here!

Last week we lived through a terrible ordeal. Monika and another young Polish girl left us forever. Olenka and I are both kind of stunned and can't quite believe that Monika, who only three days ago, was here with us laughing and joking, will never return again. She was so good and sweet, always thinking how she could help us or do something nice for us. And she was so sure that all three of us would somehow stay alive. I still see her dark smiling eyes. Both girls were very brave right up to the end. I will never forget our last evening together. I wish I could describe our mood, the expression in our eyes; although we all felt the dread, we were still capable of laughter, of light-hearted joking. We made plans to meet in Warsaw, though each of us knew, just as she did, that there was no hope of that. Today we only know that our girls were brave to the end.

Dearest parents, I write to you about this though I know that this will tear at your hearts, but I would like you to be prepared for the worst; it's better that way. Dear God, how I'd love to spare you this unhappiness, how I wish I could once again be a joy to you. Our cell, which used to be the most cheerful cell in the entire section, is now sad and quiet. No songs, no laughter. Monika was the mainstay of our trio, with her strong, deep voice. The last night that she was with us, we asked her to sing Schubert's "Ave Maria" for us.

Going through this together has brought me and Olenka closer than ever; we comfort one another as much as we can, and I think of our coming separation with such sadness. We have been close to one another from the very beginning. Olenka was arrested the day after I was. We were together at Pawiak, and we came to the Alex together.

You know what, Mummy, I read your letter to Marysia and Wanda, and then we read Marysia's mother's letters, which are so lovely and moving that we all cried over them like babies. Do you still remember my little Mimi in your prayers, Mummy? Thank you for the shampoo, which I received unopened.

I have a great favor to ask you, Daddy. Send me a package of cigarettes and some matches. Actually we can't smoke here, but just in case I must go to the place of execution, it would be nice to have one last cigarette. It would be a bit comforting, a compensation for that other difficulty.

Kisses from my raven-haired Olenka.

[unsigned]

Alt-Moabit, Berlin
June 1943[38]

I was so touched by your note, all the more because it was so unexpected. I only regret that we were never together, that I couldn't get to know your deepest thoughts. Marysia, how I would love to know more about you and reveal myself to you. From what I know of you, I am sure that we share similar thoughts and opinions.

Thank you for your poems and for taking the trouble to write them out again for me. You know, I had only read them once or twice when they found them during an inspection and took them away, and I missed them so much. You wrote to my Mimi the things you wanted her to hear. You are very dear for remembering her in your letter to me. I love Mimi and suffered Helmut's death with her, like the death of someone close to me. I would give anything to be with her and cheer her up, but I am locked up here knowing that she is suffering alone. Thank God that we [Krystyna and Olenka] are still together and don't have to worry about one another. Sometimes we weave fantastic dreams of a large cell just for Polish political prisoners where we could all be

---

38. A letter smuggled to Maria Kacprzyk.

together. What a joy that would be. Not a prison but paradise! I am so attached to Olenka, and the thought of her leaving makes me very sad. Together we loved to joke and act silly, behavior that Monika looked upon with forbearance. I tease Olenka constantly and try to arouse her envy because she won't get to Plotzensee[39] and will never get to wear a black death shroud. On this subject, we make bets, and since earthly values no longer matter to us, the loser will have to take the winner's place in purgatory.

I must go now, Marysia, because it is rapidly getting dark, but I want to copy something beautiful for you. It is an ancient German prayer that Mimi sent me. It is really beautiful, though of course, you are no longer contemplating death, dear Marysia. And though I still dream so intensely of life, I embrace you both, dear friends, because you are mine, and especially Lena[40] and raven-haired Wanda, because you share my fate.

> If someday I must leave
> Stay by me
> If I must suffer death
> Stay by me
> When my heart
> Is in the grip of terror
> Release me from fear
> Let Your strength, through Your fear and Your pain
> Be my shield
> My consolation in death
> Let me see Your countenance
> In Your suffering on the Cross
> Then I will gaze at You
> Full of faith
> Press You to my heart
> And so die in peace

---

39. Plotzensee Prison, where the executions took place.
40. Lena Dobrzycka, also sentenced to death, later a cell mate of Krystyna's.

Alt-Moabit, Berlin
July 4, 1943

Dear parents,

It's now our second Sunday without Monika. How quickly time passes within these four walls of our cell. Sometimes we can't believe it. Thank you very much for your dear letters, Mummy, and for the package of washing powder, soap, and shampoo. I received it unopened. Where did you get such fantastic soap? We smell it all day long and revel in its prewar aroma. We can assume that the fact that Daddy's petition got to the governor is a positive sign, and I am really curious what will come of it. Olenka is still with me, but we are so conscious of the fact that we must soon part. I wonder who will next be brought to my cell. It is unlikely that I would be transferred to a large cell because I have the buttonhole making machine here. It will be so lonely here without Olenka. Today in chapel, I saw Wanda, our little "golden heart" for the last time. She is leaving for a *Straflager* tomorrow. Little by little, our group is breaking up. Have you heard anything else about Olenka's mother? She [Olenka] is very concerned and feels guilty because she thinks it's because of her.[41] I feel so terrible about Karol and his parents; what will they do without him and without money? I am so pleased that things aren't too bad for you, that you, Mummy, are somehow managing. Is it true that a pair of stockings costs 800 zloty in Warsaw? Write to me about conditions in Warsaw—whether the cafés are always full like they used to be?

Olenka just received letters from home, sat down in the corner on the sofa (mattress) and is engrossed in them. I hope she doesn't end up in tears, though that is what letters from home usually do. We wanted desperately to draw a picture for you to show you how I do my hair now, so that you would have a better picture of me, but after many attempts, we came to the conclusion that our drawing abilities are not up to it, so I guess I will have to describe it to you. I have it rolled under, both sides ear length, and in front, it is waved to the back. Do you pic-

---

41. Olenka's mother was arrested and sent to a concentration camp.

ture it? My hair is now blonde only at the ends, so if you see me again, I will look as I did long ago.

Here it is as cold as in Warsaw, and I wear my skirt and blue sweater every day except Sunday, when I put on my flower-print dress. We have four chamomile flowers in a glass in our cell—the first time we have had such a thing in prison—and it seems to us that we have never seen anything so beautiful. Where is Olenka's cousin?

I am very pleased that you have made friends. I don't want time to stand still for you, dearest Mummy. I have never needed you so much as I need you now, and if I come back, then you will see how happy we will be! How is Pani Wanda feeling? Does she still look so terrible? Tell her not to worry about me. If only Zbyszek keeps his head about him (and I don't doubt that he will), then I'm sure everything will somehow turn out. Marysia told me that today you will visit her mother. Marysia is really our treasure. Olenka has finished reading her letters and has fallen asleep in the corner. How lovely she looks. I must get her to lie down because she has a cold and had a fever last night. Thank you, Mummy, for praying for all of my beloved friends. My dear little Mimi is still here, not far away, and I see her every day during *Freistund*. I wrote Zbyszek a note, but I don't know if he got it. Has he not mentioned this in his letters? Send me a bigger mirror, if you like, and also a package of "Camellia." I am so curious whether Daddy will be able to come here but I don't dare dream about this, it would be such a joy. Sometimes I get very indifferent about everything, but I know I must want to live, for your sake, and for the sake of the future. Hugs to the two Janeks and to little Kola. Best regards to Mr. and Mrs. Mierkowski and the boys, Pani Wanda, and all the aunts. I love you terribly and send great hugs and kisses.

Your Tina

Kisses from the dark-haired Olenka.

Thank you for the picture and the litany, but I don't know if I will recite it. Even prison hasn't taught me to pray long prayers, but I do believe that God does not abandon prisoners. Dear Daddy, send us some ordinary laundry soap please.

Alt-Moabit, Berlin
July 11, 1943

Beloved parents,

A moment ago, Olenka left me. She was transferred to the transport cell, and tonight she will leave for Witten-Annen in Westphalia. I am again alone in my cell. It is so strange and so lonely. Separation is not half so hard on the one who is leaving, but for the one left behind in a place just recently filled with friendship, it is much, much harder. Yesterday we spent our last evening, keeping our tradition of singing all the songs we used to sing with Monika, we danced the polka and had a good time, but this morning we glanced sadly at one another, and even our Sunday bean soup didn't taste good. One thing that pleases me is that Olenka is going to the same place Wanda went, so they might meet, and then they won't feel so lonely. During my few days alone (for I hope that I will soon get another companion), I should prepare myself for the fact that I will soon be summoned by the authorities and be told what is to happen to me, and I must be prepared for everything. I still have many other matters weighing heavily upon me. Perhaps you have already heard that Marysia will have another trial, which worries me terribly. My God, I was so pleased that at least all my girls [arrested with her] were saved.

Zbyszek wrote me a sad letter; he fears a severe sentence. He is sure that my trial is over, so he is asking me to write him the truth about everything. I don't know what to do; I'm afraid that the news will weaken his resolve just when he needs it most. Tell Pani Wanda that Zbyszek feels well and is calm. He used his allotted letter to write to me. I am also worried about Mimi, who has a painful infection in her hand, so much that she can't sleep at night. During *Freistund,* I see the dark circles under her tired eyes, but there's nothing I can do for her, only send her a kiss from a distance.

Dearest Mummy, I hope that this letter will reach you before your Name Day because I want to send you best wishes and this little handkerchief. It is so little and quite useless, but I made it thinking the whole time of you. The three flowers are symbols: yellow for Olenka, red for Monika, and blue for myself. Don't worry about a thing, Mummy, and

Handkerchief Krystyna embroidered at Alt-Moabit for her mother

I love you for writing to me so often. Catholic services are held in the prison chapel, on the fourth floor, every second Sunday. Everybody attends if they have permission from the court. I have had permission since about Easter, and some other girls have too. Beloved Daddy, you can't imagine how enthusiastically I greet your letters, each of which is guaranteed to improve my humor for at least two days. The last one was no exception, and I eagerly await the promised parcel. I will try to send you a card midweek. I am sending you excerpts from a poem written for us by an unknown author.[42]

Three little Polish children
Ever cheerful and serene
Live in cell no. 18
Berlin, Alt-Moabit.
Fate united them
Far from home and native land
They never complain
They are so brave.
They served their Polish homeland
With the best they had to offer.
They took away their freedom
And now they want their lives!
Olga's sentence was commuted
With boundless joy they thanked God
for showing his love
But one had to die—little Monika
She who was most convinced
That freedom was near.
A profound silence descended
Where once there was singing and dancing.
Soon Olga too will leave
Then Krystyna will wait all alone.
Dear God! Grant her life
I will be eternally grateful.

---

42. Mimi Terwiel.

I hope this poem will show you that we maintain a positive mood and spirit no matter what fate demands of us. Write to me, Daddy, and tell me what sort of harvest you expect this year, not only in Brwinów, but everywhere. How I'd love to walk with you through the fields. Here I can't even stick my head out the window because the bars are too close.

Kisses to you both, with special Name Day kisses for Mummy, and kindest regards to all my friends.

Your Tina

Mummy, send me my new stockings that I left in the cupboard.

Alt-Moabit, Berlin
July 24, 1943

My own, beloved Mummy,

Today is my Name Day, so I am sure you were thinking all day about your little girl so far away. This morning, while I was still sleeping, Lena[43] put your photograph on the pillow near my head, and all day it seemed to me that you were here with me. I got your package today just after dinner, and I thank you so much for all those lovely surprises. I immediately sewed a dress for my naked little doll, and I won't part with it for a moment. Lena made a handkerchief for me, embroidered with every natural and supernatural symbol of good luck, which should protect me from death!

But the finest Name Day present was the happy outcome of Marysia's trial. For several weeks, since we first heard about her retrial, I lived in a constant state of anxiety. I only found out on the morning of her trial that I too would have to go, to testify. Naturally, we were ecstatic, first of all, because it is always better to go together, and that also meant

---

43. Helena Dobrzycka, Krystyna's new cell mate.

that I would not have to wait to find out the outcome. I wasn't there for the whole thing, only at the very beginning, and then I was recalled for a few minutes to testify. The rest of the time I was in the *Arestzelle,* where prisoners wait, guarded by soldiers. You can imagine how nervous I was. I thought it would never end, though in fact it lasted three and a half hours. I caught a glimpse of Marysia returning through the courtyard. She was smiling, so I decided that things went well. On our way back, we looked so happy that our guards asked us if we were *freigesprochen* [acquitted]. They were absolutely amazed when I told them that in three months time I will be executed. I am so pleased, and it is so much easier to accept my sentence, knowing that my girls will return home.

Mummy, try to see Olenka's sister or grandmother and ask them if they have any news of her from the camp. If they can write to her, ask them to send her a kiss from me and tell them about the fortunate outcome of Marysia's trail. They should also tell her that we are now three in cell no. 18, that everything is fine except that I miss her so much. You probably don't know who Lena is and what a wonderful friend I have found in this jail. Lena spent a few months in Lomianki with her aunt and uncle Makolski, and there she was arrested last summer. This came up in our conversation just by chance. Now we are both awaiting the results of our appeals—Lena has been waiting almost six months.

Is that Daddy of mine going to come to visit? Because a lawyer came to see Marysia today and told her that her father got his permit and will soon visit her. So I got very jealous, especially since Marysia is bound to see her father someday anyway. Last Sunday was wonderful. I got such sweet letters from Pani Wanda, Aunt Bronka, and Alina, and I was especially pleased to hear about you, Mummy, that you are so fantastically courageous. I am so grateful for that, my dearest Mummy. You must persuade the two Janeks to come to you; it would be safer for them and better for you.

Pani Wanda wondered how these experiences will affect our character and disposition. It is hard to evaluate that here under these abnormal circumstances. We will only know once we are out again in a normal world. We too have discussed this, whether we will ever be able to live again like normal people. We think we will see the world through different eyes because here, living with a death sentence hanging over us, so many things have become unimportant. Anyway, we decided that when we get out we will be very fussy about choosing a husband. It can't be just anybody because few men will impress us; we have endured and learned so much.

You know, Mummy, here it is a fact that women take death sentences much more bravely, that they bear all difficulties with much more dignity, and so I am a bit conceited. But not too much.

I wrote to Zbyszek last week, and I was a bit relieved to hear from Pani Wanda that there is some hope for him.

June 25, 1943 (continued)

Back to my letter. Today is a terribly boring Sunday, we don't go to chapel or to *Freistund;* in other words, we sit all day in our cell, and we don't even work. Outside the weather is glorious and hot—in the cell, it is so hot we can't breathe. The best moment is when we can cool off a little by washing from head to toe in cold water.

I rather hope that today I will get a letter from you for my Name Day because all I got this week was a brief note. Write to me, Mummy, and tell me what Jacek is doing, and whether he is still pessimistic about the whole world and the future. How is little Eva? Give Kasia my best and tell her to get well soon. I am so pleased that you have good friends who can comfort you.

I want to thank you, in Mimi's name, for praying for her. Actually, she is a full ten years older than I, but very delicate and looks almost like a child. Her mother doesn't know she has been arrested and sentenced to death. She has a heart condition, so Mimi's brother and sister are keeping it from her, telling her that Mimi has gone to Switzerland. Consequently, Mimi gets no letters from her and misses her terribly. I am luckier in that respect and feel very sorry for her. I am getting along very well with my new cell mates, but Olenka was my favorite of the Polish girls here. Lena and I keep asking ourselves just how long we will remain together. Marysia has met several times with our lawyer, who reassured her about our situation, though he hastened to add that fate does play tricks. But don't fret about this, dearest Mummy, just keep your chin up as I do. There's lots of time for worrying, I always tell myself, and I enjoy every day as much as possible.

Kisses from the bottom of my heart, my one and only Mummy, and thank you again for the letters and parcels.

Your Tina

Dearest Alina—Your postcards are beautiful. Often in the evening I remove them from the box, set them on the table, and gaze at them. What a beautiful, incredible world they show, so different from ours. One simply forgets that somewhere there are silent, peaceful evenings. Last night Marysia woke me up to look out at the moon, which appeared through the grill, high above the prison walls.

Hugs to you and your darling babies and thanks for all your prayers. I too think of Stan.[44]

Your Tina

Alt-Moabit, Berlin
August 1, 1943

Dear little Helga,[45]

We were so moved that you sent us some apples! We were as disappointed as you that you couldn't come to us yesterday. You have no

---

44. Alina's husband, killed at the start of the war.

45. The first of Krystyna's letters to Helga Grimpe, the teenage daughter of the guard Krystyna called Sonnenschein, who smuggled their letters in and out of the prison.

idea how much it means that someone is good and kind to us. Unfortunately, not all the guards are as nice as your mother. We call your mother our "ray of sunshine" and are so happy when we see her. She just brought me a blouse for buttonholes, and I set to work with such zeal that I broke the needle.

Little Helga! You are a girl from another world, the kind we have almost forgotten, where girls live with their mothers and can come and go as they like. You can see and hear beautiful things, but we are surrounded by grey walls and all our thoughts about the future end with this question—will I live to the end of this week? Still, we try not to lose our good humor, to maintain good cheer as much as we can. We tell ourselves this is not a prison but a strict boarding school, and our guards are our horrible teachers. But we miss our country and life is sometimes unbearable thinking about our mothers who await with dread the final outcome of our appeal.

It's too bad you can't come here in the evening and stay a while. We would sing you our songs and tell you about our experiences. Many old people have not lived through as much as we have. We feel optimistic today and talk about being out and going to a café with our little friend Helga. We would eat cakes until we almost burst, and on top of that, I would chain-smoke ten cigarettes.

Don't laugh at my faulty German, but I only studied it during the war. All the best from the three of us.

Krystyna, Maria, Lena

I am enclosing two addresses, one in Warsaw and the other for our estate, where we hope to return after the war. One of these is sure to be good, but try the one in Warsaw first.

Krystyna Wituska or K. Wituska
63b Wspólna Street, Apt. 5
Malyn Post Office
Warsaw
Majątek Jerzew, Poland

Alt-Moabit, Berlin
August 5, 1943

Dear Helga,

The apples were delicious. We gobbled them up very quickly for fear of getting caught, and destroyed your letter immediately.

Essigsaure Tonerde—Acetate Slime—isn't that a fantastic nickname? We racked our brains for the longest time and nothing could be more appropriate. From now on we shall never call her anything else, but you can imagine how careful we must be. They're always eavesdropping. She spies on us all the time and once said to me: "If I had a daughter like you, I would go crazy." Thank God, I thought, that she has no children. They would be tormented mercilessly.

Your letter helped ease the deep sorrow that has enveloped us since yesterday. Yesterday my dearest friend [Mimi], who was in my cell for a long time at the Alex, was taken away to Barnimstrasse.[46] She was sentenced to death six months ago, so I am so afraid for her, and what depresses me most is that there is no way to find out whether she is still alive or not.

Do the air raids frighten you, Helga? Won't you get away from Berlin during this dangerous time? To enable us to protect ourselves in the event of an American bomb hitting here, we now get our washbasin and food bowl filled with water every evening.[47]

On Sunday we saw your beautiful dress. We think you will look splendid when you step out. If it weren't for my anxiety for my friend, we would be feeling quite good right now, but even when things are bad, we never show it. No one here must ever so much as think that they have defeated us.

My sentence has still not been ratified (touch wood three times!). It would be terrible to get killed just before the end of the war. I have

---

46. The administrative center through which prisoners passed when their sentences were carried out, whether to another penal institution or execution.

47. Presumably the water was supplied in case of fire, though clearly Krystyna saw how ridiculous it was to think that a bowl of water would put out a fire caused by a bomb.

„Essigsaure Tonerde"

Drawing of the hated guard Krystyna and her friends named *Essigsaure Tonerde*
("Acetate Slime")

to stop now, Helga, before the guard notices that my sewing machine is silent. How awful it is to know that I can be observed at any time through the peep-hole. Unfortunately, most of the time they are not your mother's eyes but those of the other "aunties"[48] peering into our cell lest we be doing something forbidden. Once again, thank you and best regards,

Krystyna W.

Alt-Moabit, Berlin
August 9, 1943

Dear little Helga,

Despite the rain outside, we had a bright day here. Sonnenschein dropped in several times, and on her last visit she brought your letter and some marvelous apples. You know, as soon as I'm out of here, I will invite you to Poland, where my parents have a large estate with lots and lots of fruit trees. You see how nervy I am—a death sentence hanging over my head and I plan for the future. You know what else we like to do when we are on our pallets? We plot our escape! If only we had a file to cut the bars on the window, etc. We picture the look on the face of the guard when she walks in and finds the cell empty; the thought of it makes us laugh. For the time being, however, we are very much stuck here. It is still light outside, but here it is "evening," since we ate supper long ago (gloppy cereal). I never fail to be impressed by your lovely writing paper—I'm so used to using just any scrap of paper.

Are you feeling better, Helga? Sonnenschein told us you weren't well and couldn't sleep last night. I too can't sleep, but for a different reason. I'm so worried about my friend. If only I knew if she is still alive!

---

48. A nickname for all the guards.

What's a Planetarium? I don't know that word. It must be something wonderful since you want to take me there. I can't find the rabbit—it must be a joke, just to catch people.[49]

Best regards from your—Krysia, Marysia, and Lena

Alt-Moabit, Berlin
August 10, 1943

Beloved little Mummy,

Today I got your card dated July 27, and the parcel containing cotton wool, and a pretty collar. Please don't send me any food because that causes more harm than good. Besides, that's really not important, I'm not hungry anyway. I'm sure you were worried because I hadn't written for so long, but a lot happened last week, and I had a hard time collecting my thoughts. You must have heard the good news about Zbyszek's verdict. I can imagine Pani Wanda's happiness, much as mine. Two days after his trial we met and could talk a little longer. Zbyszek was beaming with joy and I was happy to see that he looked quite well, which he certainly didn't at the Alex. He was also quite pleased with how I looked.

Mummy, they took my little Mimi away and I don't know where, but I suspect the worst. If you knew how much I came to love her, you would realize how much this hurts me. Anyway, no matter what, we must hold our heads high, just like Mimi did, to the end!

Stay calm, dear little Mummy, I am really not afraid. If only I could reassure you somehow. Thank everyone in Borowin for the card they sent me on my Name Day. It was so sweet of them. Kisses to Pani Wanda and Alina, and regards to Mr. and Mrs. Mierkowski. And most of all, a kiss for you, my best Mummy.

Your Tina

---

49. Probably referring to some kind of a riddle drawing.

Alt-Moabit, Berlin
August 14, 1943

Dear Helga,

This will be my last letter to you for now because Sonnenschein is leaving us for a while. Will there ever be another good week like this one? We will feel like orphans. I wonder what kind of witch will replace her. You are a sweet girl, Helga, and your letter saved me from a flood of tears; Sonnenschein told me that Mimi was dead. It's better that I know, though it will be very hard for me to get used this thought, and I will never get over this loss. I console myself that Mimi is no longer suffering. What a shame, a terrible shame, that such a good, talented human being had to die such a horrible death.

You probably know that we got lots of mail today, including the news that my father received permission for a fifteen-minute visit. I'm so afraid that I will get too emotional and not be able to say a word. After all, I must show him I am brave and up to any situation. They are already suffering too much.

Pity that the idea of the gramophone is impossible. We miss music so much. Yesterday we could hear someone playing a piano; we sat motionless, deeply moved. Where did it come from? At that moment I realized how much of the world's beauty has been taken away from us.

Your letter from the air raid shelter was so shocking. It's much easier for us. We are ordered to get dressed but since it's completely dark and nobody can see anything, we might, at best, put on a skirt and calmly go back to sleep. We only regret that we must black out our windows because it would be interesting—bright rockets and colorful bombs.

I will ask for the book that you want on Monday (our book day). I will probably be able to get it. The weather is getting nicer. I'm sure you will be able to enjoy some fresh air on Sunday.

If they take me away, Helga, I will write one last letter to you. I will leave it with Marysia if Sonnenschein is not here. And when they have killed me, I will float like a fat little angel on a cloud above your house to see what you are doing. We are very careful with the letters, Helga, because we know how dangerous it is for your mother. I will tell you a secret. Mimi and I exchanged more than 200 letters without getting caught. Prisoners are so carefully watched, and yet still find ways to communicate. The guards are cunning, so we are more cunning—that is our motto. Before inspections, we hide everything so well that even we can't find it later.

Good night, Helga, it's completely dark now and we have no lights. All the best,

Your Krystyna

Alt-Moabit, Berlin
August 15, 1943

Hello [to Helga]!

Sonnenschein told us what happened last night. What a loss. I am so sorry and furious that this happened to your mother.[50] She's so sweet though, that despite everything, she still brought us a bag of tomatoes and apples. Let's hope that her things are recovered.

Through our window we see only a bit of sky, however, it's enough for us to observe all sorts of wonderful clouds. Often I stand by the window, gaze at the sky, and long for freedom. I select for myself a special cloud. Helga, you are your mother's greatest treasure. Because she has you, all her sorrows are bearable. Stay as lovable as you are.

Your Krystyna

Alt-Moabit, Berlin
August 15, 1943

My dearest Mummy,

Yesterday I got your letter, scolding me for not writing for such a long time and wondering whether a letter of mine had been confiscated

---

50. Mrs. Grimpe was robbed during an air raid.

by the censors. It's just that last Sunday, I wrote to Mimi's brother and sister, and the Sunday before, to Zbyszek.[51] You and Pani Wanda must be so happy about Zbyszek's verdict; what good fortune. I didn't even dare dream it could turn out this way. I saw him that day; such a pleasant surprise, but that was also the day Mimi left us, so I had to force myself to appear in good humor. Mimi is gone forever, like the other girls. The only comfort is that all the evil things are behind her now; she will no longer suffer and long for her beloved Helmut. Now I finally realize what it means to lose someone you love, forever!

I also got a card from Daddy yesterday and he writes about visiting me soon. I am delirious with joy but I am still afraid to believe it, I can't believe it is really possible. But now I will wait for this every day. We heard from little Wanda from the *Straflager*; she is with Olenka and their work is hard but clean. It is a camp for Polish women only and there are seventy-two of them. I gather from their letter that they are not doing too badly. It would be good if Marysia were sent there too. You must know that she is in my cell, along with Lena Dobrzycka, about whom you've probably heard from Mrs. Makolska—if you get to see her. Both of them look well and are in good health. I am now sort of a *Stubenalteste* [head girl in the cell] because I speak German best and I feel like the oldest, though in fact there is no difference in age between Lena and me. Halinka is awful for not wanting to be with you,[52] although, who knows, under the circumstances, maybe I too would prefer to stay with my husband if I loved him. At this moment, I just got your letter dated the 2nd in which you write about Olenka. Thank Pani Wanda for her card. Perhaps I will write her a few words, but at the moment I don't feel up to writing a letter. Forgive me, but I must finish now.

I love you and thank you for writing so often. Give my best to everyone.

Your Tina

---

51. Krystyna was permitted only one letter per week.

52. She wanted her sister to move to Warsaw so their mother would not be alone. No doubt Halinka remained in the country with her small child because it was safer.

Secret letter to
Helga on official
prison stationery

Alt-Moabit, Berlin
August 17, 1943

Gelesen _____ [53]

To be signed by: Sonnenschein

Today was, without question, the most unbelievably happy day. My
head still can't fully absorb that fact that today I actually saw my father.
Looking at him sitting across from me, I felt that my year in prison and
my death sentence were just a bad dream. I managed to maintain my
happy disposition the whole time he was here, Helga, and I am sure

---

53. This letter to Helga, written on official prison stationery, jokingly instructs Sonnenschein to sign it in the space following Gelesen, meaning "read by."

that my father left me convinced that I am getting along here very well. He even managed to exchange a few words with our Sonnenschein, and that reassured him that I am getting good care here. Unfortunately, they took away the sweets, the cigarettes, and the flowers he brought me. But that doesn't matter! During our conversation, he expressed the hope that before too long, we will be able to return to our family estate in Wartheland, our home from which the Germans evicted us. But it is not the estate that is important, but only that we are all together at last. I gave him Mimi's family's address and asked him to go see them and give them my kindest regards. The only thing, it was such a short visit and there was so much to say. I want to believe that someday I will be able to tell him about everything. And oh, I was able to hug him! How comforting that was.

Later in the afternoon I had a visit from our lawyer, a totally pointless visit. He lectured me a lot about hope and apologized for not greeting me during Maria's trial, but it is forbidden to communicate with people sentenced to death. What a laugh! I told him so.

Now about your letter: You are a marvelous girl. We positively cheered on discovering that you think as we do. You know, I practically faint when I read in the newspapers about "holy hatred" and revenge—against me, I suppose, since I am one of the enemies of the Reich who must be liquidated. So they must get their revenge by cutting off my head! I sometimes think that they won't grant me clemency simply because things are going quite badly for them, so they'll think they can't afford the luxury of being so magnanimous. I don't care! Dear, dear Helga, I am sorry if I've made you unhappy with my letter. I didn't mean to. We *Kleeblatter* [cloverleaves][54] are so used to talking about death, we think it's a perfectly natural, normal topic for conversation. I forget that for others, it might be depressing. In fact, today my pleasant neighbor and I carried on a great philosophical discussion of precisely this topic during our daily walk. The guard was gracious enough not to disturb us.

Yesterday, a cigarette fell from the heavens. I smoked it in the evening. To be honest, it made me feel a little ill, it's been so long since I've

---

54. A term she often used for the three women in her cell.

had one. But it was splendid!

I have to stop now because it's getting too dark. But I'm too agitated to fall asleep—my father is still in Berlin. His train leaves at eleven.

Lena and Maria send their thanks for your kind words, and we all wish you and our Sonnenschein a peaceful night, without air raids.

Best regards from your *Kleeblatt*.

[Note in the margin] Hello again. Just a few words while waiting for Sonnenschein to come. We still have the little dog.[55] He has such a funny expression on his face, we can't help but laugh. My wish, that you would have a night without an air raid, alas, did not come true.

Alt-Moabit, Berlin
August 18, 1943

Dearest Father,

I hope you returned home in good health and in good spirits. Now you no longer have to worry, having seen for yourself how well I'm doing. The person, Sonnenschein, whom you chanced to see is very sweet and lovable. Pity you couldn't speak to her. I am very curious—did you get a chance to meet and speak to Gerd and Ursel,[56] and do they know yet what happened to Mimi? Are they grieving terribly? You absolutely must write and tell me everything. I loved that girl so much. She was the best companion imaginable—so gifted, good humored, and always ready to help others. I'd like to have a sister like that. Losing Mimi has been a terrible blow for me.

Our court-appointed lawyer was here yesterday and gave me a long lecture about hope. All day I've been in high spirits and people were admiring my radiant face.

---

55. A mascot made out of rags.
56. Mimi Terwiel's brother and sister.

Cover and first page of Helga's album
containing Krystyna's letters

Cristina Wituska †
Gelebt als Mensch /geadelt
zur Heldin durch bitterliches
Leiden /geendet als Heilige
für die Freiheit Polens!

You are a wonderful person. Despite all your difficulties, you got here. Too bad I couldn't keep the cigarettes and the sweets. But that is not important. The main thing, I always say, is my mental state. Keep well and bravely hold your head high, no matter what happens.

Heartfelt kisses to you both and to Michael.[57]

Your Tina

Alt-Moabit, Berlin
August 18, 1943

Dear Helga,

In your letter you mentioned Sonnenschein's fattening treatment. You know, I'm worried that if this keeps up I will lose my slender silhouette! When I was at the Alex with Mimi, we really starved, so it's no wonder that I'm not fat. How overjoyed we were when one of the cleaning women, who couldn't chew because of her dentures, took pity on us and gave us her bread crusts. Still, despite the hunger and the cold at the Alex, I remember those days as a special time. Mimi and I were together in a tiny cell, and just to spite them, we laughed constantly. Tonight, if I have time, I will tell you more about our life at the Alex. I didn't get the books. They gave me three books that I've already read. My father is now in Warsaw.

All the best,

Your Krystyna.

---

57. Relationship unknown.

Alt-Moabit, Berlin
August 18, 1943

Dear Helga,

Sonnenschein just came in to say goodnight and once again brought us some splendid cakes. Helga, you have no idea what a golden heart your mother has. You'll never understand how much her dear heart—not to mention those cakes!—mean to us.

We now have a new guard, an awful blonde woman, and all day long we hear her resounding voice bellowing in the corridors. We call her Bazyliszek,[58] the name of a dragon in a children's story who could kill just with his glance. She really does have the most horrible eyes. When we are out for our walk, we must look straight ahead and we can't smile, or else she sends us immediately back to our cell. She is always very self-important—must be working for a promotion.

Today, right after supper, I heard a victorious cry from the neighboring cell: "The army has retreated from Sicily!" Unfortunately, we had no champagne, only water, or else I would have got royally drunk—to ease our sorrow, of course. What a shame that Mimi is not here to hear this.

Now I must tell you something about the Alex. The cells were very small with only a narrow cot and a stool. Nothing else; in any case there was no room left for anything. We sat all day on the cot wrapped in a blanket. It was terribly cold; they never heated the place. We had to sleep together on the one cot; it was uncomfortable but it kept us a bit warmer. We had to share the bed with a great extended family of bedbugs. The walls were wet and sticky. Nobody cared about us, and we could have died three times before anyone would have noticed that we had hoisted a flag.[59] But it was better that way. At least we were left in peace. We could have hidden a machine gun under our beds. Our cell was so lice infested, none of the guards ever stepped inside. There were no inspections. We could stand all day at the windows and talk to our

---

58. Krystyna also refers to this hated guard, Bauer, as "the Dragon" in her letters.
59. They kept a Polish flag hidden under the cot.

Krystyna's letter to
Helga signed with the
cloverleaf

neighbors. Although that wasn't so easy since only the top ventilator
was open. We had to balance on our toes on the edge of the window
in order to get our heads out. After a while, I got used to this unusual
posture and could hang there for hours—except after supper when I'd
get a belly like Buddha's, in which case I'd soon feel quite ill. We had a
fantastic postal service organized there. Using a long pole to open the
ventilators, we passed around books, newspapers, cigarettes, bread, even
bowls of soup. The windows were so close together that it was quite easy
to reach. We also established contact with the men, who were on the
floor below us. Using a rope, we managed to lower bowls of soup because the Gestapo often deprived them of it. Sometimes a tragedy—the
string broke and everything landed on the ground in the courtyard below. What a loss for a starving man. When we had no string, we tied our
stockings and handkerchiefs together. All this was done after dark. We

lived on the fifth floor. Sometimes, when we shouted from one window to another, Schup would call out from the courtyard, "Quiet up there!" And everything would be quiet—for about five minutes.

To be continued. It's dark again.

All the best,

Your [signed with a drawing of a cloverleaf, the initials—C: Christine, M: Maria, L: Lena—in each segment of the leaf.]

Alt-Moabit, Berlin
Sometime in late August 1943

Dear Helga,

I am sure you've spent a pleasant Sunday with your Mummy. We are delighted with your letters from Turingen; it's nice of you not to forget us even while you're away. We laughed at your Nazi "friend." Today we're hungry like wolves. I've searched the cell, but there's nothing here apart from soap and toothpaste. Pity. You'd better wait until I've finished telling you my story before you decide whether you'd like to join us.

My friendship with Mimi was the bright light of my miserable prison life; everybody who knew her will not easily forget her. She was splendid, so talented, good humored, and always ready to help others. She was a lawyer and very musical. They couldn't break her.

At the Alex, after she was sentenced to death, Gestapo officers frequently appeared at the cell to say they were coming to take her to Plotzensee. Maniacs that they were, they thought this was a joke—they wanted the pleasure of frightening her. But she never reacted and each time they left sorely disappointed. It was here, at Moabit, that she finally became very depressed, when they took away her fiancé. She loved him terribly and—something rare—he was worthy of her love. That's when I really worried about her, that in her grief, she might do something. I was the only one who knew what she was going through at this time. Whenever she went out of the cell, it was always with a smile. She was too proud to reveal her pain. I often ask myself: What will happen to a nation that murders its best people?

I'm afraid that this letter will depress you again, but it is impossible to write only cheerful letters from a prison. Besides, you said I could express whatever I feel. I don't think one should know only pleasant things; one must know everything that is going on. Not many people in Berlin realize how many men and women are confined in these cells, how many executions are carried out each day. We are once again in shock—seven French and Belgian women, among them Mimi's friend,[60] were taken away to Barnimstrasse.

You know, you're right, Marysia is a melancholy girl. I worry about her and will be relieved when she is taken out of here and sent to the penal camp.

On Saturday, we got the most wonderful surprise. Our sweet, cheerful neighbor [Jutta] was sentenced to only eight years in prison. She expected a death sentence. An absolute miracle! She has a five-year-old daughter and dark, laughing eyes.

Do you know how to tap dance, Helga? I learned it in jail. In Alexanderplatz, where we could barely move a few steps, Mimi gave me tap dancing lessons. Of course that only made us hungrier, but at least we didn't freeze. Ivan, the Ukrainian below us, nearly went mad from the noise of our exercises. Two cells away was a dancer who also exercised a lot. She was very conceited and boasted to everyone that she was composing a ballet titled *The Last Interrogation*. Interrogations at the Alex were unpleasant; mine lasted sometimes from five to seven hours. Always the same questions and the same threats; when I got back to my cell, I would shake from nervous exhaustion. I was unusually lucky that they didn't beat me. None of my cell mates were so fortunate. There were lots of attempted suicides at the Alex—people simply couldn't stand the interrogations. Sometimes people jumped over the metal railing of the fifth floor landing, killing themselves on the stone floor below.

---

60. Rita Arnould, a Belgian Jew.

Mimi and I often talked about suicide. She said that she could not wait patiently like a sheep until they decided to kill us. For a long time we considered this, but finally decided that we must leave to them the moral responsibility for our murder.

Thank God this boring Sunday is finally over; they gave us those same boring books again. That drives me crazy. My sweet neighbor[61] was moved to Section II. I nearly cried. We were the two oldest residents of this wing, and I had got so attached to her. For the time being at least, she is in the cell above us, and we can talk through the window, only I'll never be able to see her again. Helga, you have no idea how important windows are in prison. If the guards only knew . . .

In my mind I can see Sonnenschein's beaming face, a vision that always has such a positive effect on us.

We wish you sunny and happy days during your holiday. Best wishes from,

Your Cloverleaf

Alt-Moabit, Berlin
August 22, 1943

Dear Pani Wanda,

You were once interested in the effect that prison life has had on my disposition and my character. I now have a strange desire to tell you about this, what my thoughts are at this time. Perhaps that is because it seems to me that you will understand this best, and you will see it objectively—not like Mummy, who is blinded by her great love for me. I wish to be very sincere. Now that some of your anxiety is eased about Zbyszek, I'm not afraid that I would add to your worries.

Maybe this is completely unnecessary, but I would like someone to know more about me, though in the end, it really doesn't matter. It's hard to write this because it's hard, almost impossible, to find the words

---

61. Unidentified.

to describe all these contradictory thoughts and feelings. Every time I think about Zbyszek, I feel an immense debt of gratitude to fate that he was saved. I doubt that my death will have any long-term effect on his life in the future; he is so young. I know now from my own experience how quickly a person can accept and get used to things that at first seem impossible to bear.

Thinking about Mummy's despair is far more painful for me than abandoning all my plans for the future, but there's nothing I can do for her. I know that she will never forget this, but I hope that she will not break down, that she will find comfort in religion, in her love for Halinka and her grandson. It will be so hard for her; her love for me is without bounds.

I wouldn't want to exploit the idea that I am a patriot who died for her country. For one thing, I was initially propelled into the conspiracy by curiosity and a sense of adventure. Only later by love of my country. Still, I do not regret a single step I took, not even now.

However, I did not become a nationalist here, quite the contrary. I consider strong nationalism to be a serious limitation, and I always consider myself first a human being and only then a Pole. On the day that I will die, I would prefer to tell myself that I am dying for freedom and justice, rather than that I die just for my own Poland. Consciousness of a universal humanity will comfort me. But please don't misunderstand—it is not that I don't love my country, but I would relinquish my country's objectives if they were not also good for all of Europe and all of humanity.

I am not distressed that I must die. We all know that we must die; the difference is that most people don't know when their hour will come. Death is as natural as life, and that is how one should approach it. If you have a good understanding of life, you know how to accept death. The important thing is to maintain one's human dignity to the end, not to give in at the last moment to an animal-like survival instinct, not to be frightened by that moment of physical pain. But I am sure that we can overcome that, we must summon all our strength for that. We will die free, so free—because prison life taught us to detach ourselves from the minor things that enslave people on the outside. Nobody can imprison our souls unless we ourselves lock them behind the bars of narrow prejudice.

In prison I became—how awful!—much less religious. That is rather odd, but I can't be religious just because there is no other way out. I would think it presumptuous to ask God to save my life, which after all is of no great importance in the universal scheme of things. Why should I have a greater right to life than those millions who have already perished in this terrible war? What will come next, I can't and don't try to imagine. I do believe, though, that the best and the most noble that is in us will not perish, that through this we will unite with something greater than ourselves, that we will approach perfection. It is nice to think that I will meet, in another world, all those I have loved—after all, is it possible that such a powerful feeling as love could just cease to be? Yet to be completely free, one must not love individually but dedicate one's life to the greater common good. But that is for exceptional people, not for me. Because I loved Mimi too much, I now suffer unnecessarily. I can't forget my little Mimi, I can't get over her death even though I have known so many others who were killed.

I have read over my letter and all my conclusions, after so many long months of thinking, struck me as a collection of platitudes. What I had to do was to arrive at some kind of personal philosophy for my daily use. I had to find a way to achieve this objective: not to lapse into despair, not to lose our spirit even under the most tragic circumstances, and to comfort others. As for death, it is a great comfort to know that when we are gone from this earth, nothing will end or change. The sun will continue to shine, the flowers will blossom, autumn will follow summer, everything will be as it should, and always will, be. What value is one life? Today, it has the least value of anything.

Dear Pani Wanda, please believe me that I accept my fate without fear. I am well, and my father's visit gave me great joy. Please kiss all my dear aunts for me, also Pan Lucjan[62] and the boys, and I hope that Róża,[63] whom I barely know, will get well and return to Warsaw soon. Heartfelt kisses,

Tina

---

62. Dr. Lucjan Walc, Zbyszek's father.
63. Zbyszek's brother's fiancée.

Alt-Moabit, Berlin
August 29, 1943

Dearest Mummy,

It's been two weeks since any of us has received a letter from home. Were it not for Father's visit in the meantime, we would be very concerned. Perhaps it's only because the censors are holding the letters longer than usual.

Your parcel, with the box of "Camellias," arrived this week. Thank you. I need laundry powder and toothpaste. Otherwise, there is absolutely nothing new here, so much so that there's really nothing to write about. The last interesting thing was Daddy's visit of over two weeks ago. There are occasional air-raid alarms at night, but there's been only one big air raid. During the alarms we have to get up, get dressed, and the doors are unlocked, closed only with the latch. At night, all the buckets, cups, and bowls we have in our cells are filled with water so that we can protect ourselves in case of fire.

Sometimes I have a lot of work, other times less, but never so much that it tires me—and I am still in good health. We are starting to sew heavier dresses though we still make light blouses. Everything we make is for *Bombenbeschadigte* [relief for bombing victims]. We had really good food this week, that is, once we got bread with our soup and today, Sunday, apart from the pea soup, we also got a cup of rhubarb compote. In about two weeks I will see Zbyszek again because we see him every four weeks [for cross-interrogation], so I can have the pleasure of looking forward to that.

And how do you feel, Mummy? You probably worry and don't sleep at night, and I can't go and comfort you. Alas! Do you realize you will soon see your little grandson? I still think about Mimi all the time and it hurts so much. I must learn to accept something that mere human will can't change.

Kisses from the bottom of my heart my one and only dearest Mummy. Give my regards to everyone, especially Pani Wanda and Alina.

Your Tina

Alt-Moabit, Berlin
September 4, 1943

Dear Helga,

Many, many thanks for your loving letters from Gerd;[64] they were so interesting and amusing that we read them several times, and we were sorry when we had to hide them again. Last night there was a terrific air raid, and so I am quite on edge. I expect that our Sonnenschein, healthy and beaming as always, will soon appear. We heard that some of our guards were killed in the bombardment. As we listened to the thundering noise, we prayed, "Dear God, don't let the good people get killed." Really, we have never lived through anything like it. The window was open as usual, and we could see the blood-red sky and hear the ceaseless roar of the planes and the explosion of the bombs. No, we weren't afraid, just a little nervous, though for appearances sake, we pretended to be calm and even joked. But for one moment we were frightened when we could smell a strong, strange odor, and Maria said, "Gas!" Now I know that it was only the smell of phosphorous. I can't believe they would use this terrible weapon in this war; surely that's out of the question. It would be suicide for Europe, since the English and the Americans possess the best known chemicals.

This morning the prison was full of smoke spread here from the raging fires; ashes and cinders continue to float through the air. We are dying of curiosity and can hardly wait for Sonnenschein to come with some news. Through the windows, people exchange fantastic stories, each more unbelievable than the next. (Hurray! Hurray! I hear Sonnenschein.) They're saying, for example, that today we won't get any dinner. I had no sooner accepted this terrible blow—with great stoicism—when I heard the sound of the food wagon outside.

And more news this evening—the Americans have landed at Calabria. Complete madness here. I can hardly keep from laughing when I think that we Poles are not permitted any newspapers, and I receive two of them: *Lokal-Anzeiger,* delivered from the first floor on a rope, and

---

64. Mimi's brother.

Volkischer Beobachter, which is slipped to me every day when I am out for my walk. Our information services are quite well organized, don't you think?

Ah, that Sonnenschein once again brought us a bowl of potato soup; once again I can hardly bend. With my tummy bigger than Buddha's, how can I maintain a very refined posture? My roommates are laughing at me!

We read your letter of September 2. Those shorthand symbols look like nothing more than funny little crawling insects. I can't make it out at all. As for your conversation with the director of a group of girls, I must consider this a little; I have always thought that people who hold such political opinions can't be decent. Before the war maybe, but now, definitely not. People would have to be completely deaf and blind not to notice such criminality.

Imagine! I just got some heather from a Polish forest in a package from my mother. What an aroma! I was no less happy than you as I buried my nose in those fragrant purple flowers. Marysia's sentence has been confirmed.[65] She'll soon be leaving. The thought of that fills me with sadness, which is totally selfish of me. Maria is very precious, clever, and prudent. I will miss her terribly.

Well, I must finish now, dear Helga. Keep well. All the best.

Your Tina

Alt-Moabit, Berlin
September 5, 1943

My dearest Mummy,

After all this time your card dated August 5 and letter dated August 15 finally arrived, along with Halina's card from Trombowla. Our letters must now take some longer route, and we can't even dream of mail service like before. Can't thank you enough, dearest Mummy, for the

---

65. Marysia had been sentenced to eight years in a concentration camp, though the prosecutor had demanded death.

Kochana moja Mamusiu!

Po długiej, długiej przerwie nadeszła nareszcie Twoja kartka z 5/8 i list z 15/8, a także kartka z Trembowli od Halinki. Listy nasze muszą odbywać teraz dalszą drogę, dlatego o tak szybkiej korespondencji jak dawniej nie można nawet marzyć. Niewiem jak Ci dziękować Kochana Mamusiu za paczuszki, w ostatnim tygodniu dostałam dwie, w pierwszej był proszek do zębów, szampony, 3 jabłuszka i cukierki, a w drugiej ten wmos, który mi sprawił taką szaloną radość, pudełeczko z boczkiem i cukierki. Doręczono mi wszystko, dlatego że było tego niedużo, nigdy nie przysyłaj mi większych ilości jak teraz Mamusiu, wogóle uważam, że jesteś genialna w swoich pomysłach i najbardziej Kochaną Mamusią pod słońcem! Wobec tego postanowiłam się zrewanżować i przysłać Ci mój portret. Jak Ci się podoba? Ten obrazek musi Ci niestety tymczasem wystarczyć. Wyobrażam sobie, jak się tam wszyscy o nas martwicie, gdy czytacie wiadomości o nalotach.

My jesteśmy jeszcze trochę pod wrażeniem tego ostatniego, w nocy z 3-4 września. Najbardziej go odczuliśmy, bo jego celem była także nasza dzielnica. Żadna z nas się nie boi, bo ostatecznie nie mamy nic do stracenia, ale pewne wrażenie zawsze wywiera. Teren naszego więzienia zupełnie nie ucierpiał. Następnego dnia byłyśmy trochę niewyspane, ale zato dostałyśmy wyjątkowe dobre jedzenie i czujemy się znów doskonale. Nie wyobrażasz sobie, jak tutaj wspaniale zorganizowana jest pomoc

Die Untersuchungsgefangene Christina Wituska — czyli Twoja Tina.

Letter to her mother with "self-portrait"

two parcels I got last week. In the first there were toothpowder, shampoo, three apples, and candies; in the second the heather, which gave me such intense joy, a tin of bacon, and some candy. They let me keep it all because there wasn't so very much. Never send larger quantities than this. I am convinced that your gift ideas are ingenious, and, in fact, you are the best mother under the sun. Therefore I decided to return the favor and send you a self-portrait. How do you like it? I am afraid that for the time being, this is the best you can get.

I can imagine how worried you all are about us as you read about the bombing. We are still a little unsettled by the last one, the night of September 3–4. We felt it more because it was targeting this district. We are not afraid though, because we have nothing to lose, but nevertheless, it has quite an impact. The prison grounds were not hit. The next day we were a bit sleepy, but then we got better than usual food, and so we feel great. You wouldn't believe how well organized the assistance program for bombing victims is.

The heather is beside me and smells of the forest. Do you know how you say heather in German? *Erika.* Pretty, don't you think? I was so happy to hear that Karol is alive![66] I was so afraid that we would never see him again. Don't you know anything else about him? Where is he? In the east or in the west? Was he taken away for forced labor? This is all very sad for his parents, but he'll survive his exile. How I wish I knew what will become of him, what kind of person he will be in future.

And now to answer your questions: black woolen sweaters, blue shoes, and wool stockings were delivered to me at the Alex. I gave the woolen sweater to Cezara [Dickstein]. Cezara was my beloved "prison mummy." She came with me from Pawiak[67] to the Alex, and for the first two weeks we shared a cell. She was awfully kind and took such care of me. She had nothing warm with her and was freezing, while I had three pairs of warm underwear. Tell Janka Parys's aunt about her—she was her friend at the Red Cross. I gave Zbyszek the woolen socks, and the shoes to someone else—they were, in any case, five sizes too big for me, and I looked rather like a Puss 'n Boots. Don't think just because of this,

---

66. No details. Later he disappeared again.
67. The main prison in Warsaw.

that I gave all my things away. I have everything I need, but a lot of stuff in jail is a heavy load. Besides, I never expected to spend another winter in prison. What a strange coincidence—Aunt Danglowa[68] was for some time in the cell beside me. You know, she is Aunt Krysia's first cousin. I saw her once at the Alex as well. She is awfully nice and all the Polish girls call her "Auntie." Unfortunately she has been sent away to a prison in Charlottenburg.

Please wish Kola a belated but very sincere happy birthday, and thank Halinka for thinking of me. Marysia's sentence has been ratified; it will be sad to part. I should be used to these separations by now, but it's too hard. If only she could have gone to the same camp as Olenka and Wanda. I am trying again to get to see Zbyszek. Be of good cheer, by dearest Mummy. Your daughter is always smiling and cheerful.

Kisses with all my heart.

Your Tina

Best regards to Mr. and Mrs. Mierkowski. Kisses to Alina. I got the mirror. Many thanks.

Berlin
September 7, 1943

Dear Ursel and Gerd,[69]

I received your letter only on September 6. Thank you for remembering me even during your grief. For that I am very grateful. I had already learned earlier that Maria is no longer alive, though I was not

---

68. Felicja Danglowa was arrested in the fall of 1942; she was first in Pawiak (Warsaw), then Alt-Moabit, and finally in Fordon Prison in Bydgoszcz, one of the largest and harshest prisons for women. Most of the 5,700 women incarcerated there between 1939 and 1945 were Polish.

69. This letter and others to Mimi Terwiel's sister and brother, Ursel and Gerd, were written after Mimi's execution and were smuggled out by the faithful Sonnenschein. Krystyna sometimes refers to Mimi here by her formal name, Maria.

able to find out the exact date of her execution. I had no idea that she was killed the very day that she was taken away from here.

I was most pleased by that part of your letter in which you tell me that this misfortune did not break you. I expected as much from Mimi's siblings. Let us hope that she sees all this from above and is very pleased. Nor did Mimi's death weaken me. Quite the contrary. After the first terrible shock of pain passed, I determined that I would follow in my beloved friend's footsteps and bear it as bravely as she. Tears don't help anyone and besides, Mimi no longer needs sympathy; she remains now an inspiration because she died heroically for her ideals. My friends often used to say, "We can't imagine what Krystyna will do when she loses Maria." But whenever I feel like crying, I remind myself of her words: "Kryscha, don't break, don't look unhappy. Don't give them that satisfaction." Then I raise my head and I say, "No, Mimi, I won't break. I will spite them and laugh in their faces." Oh, if only my good, dear parents didn't suffer so! Sometimes, when my situation seems hopeless, I feel so sorry that they didn't let me die with Mimi. Then we would have gone to our deaths with a smile, and we would have shown them how much contempt we have for our judges and our executioners. Unfortunately, like Maria and Helmut, every one of us must take the last, terrible steps alone, abandoned. We die comforted, however, by the certainty that victory will be ours; that we didn't fight in vain for freedom.

Maria used to greet every bit of political news with great interest. Nothing delighted me more than to have some news to share with her. Right up to the end she and I would spin all kinds of fantastic plans for the future, and she avidly studied English. I marveled at her indescribable enthusiasm.

I want to tell you at least some of the things I know about Maria's life in prison; I think I could talk about her for hours, and if I ever get out of jail, I will. I promised her that the last time I saw her. But since I don't entertain great hopes that this will happen, and each day I fear that they will come for me, I am enclosing these cards I got from Maria. If I live, I will want them back, but in the meantime I want you to have them for safekeeping. There's one request I want to make: how I'd love to have a larger photograph of Maria; I have just one little snapshot. It's one that Helmut used to carry with him, and after his death, Maria gave it to me. If my appeal is turned down, I will send both photos back to you. Please grant me this favor.

Three weeks ago my father came to visit me. I gave him your address and asked him to go right away and visit you and give you my warmest personal greetings. I haven't heard yet whether he did. This letter does not go through the censors, but when you write to me, tell me only that you were pleased to get greetings from Maria . . . [fragment missing]

These are the only letters of Maria's that are still in my possession. We used to write to one another every evening and exchange the cards during our evening walk. I had more than a hundred of them, but unfortunately, I destroyed most of them for fear of their discovery during a search. The remaining ones are in a dreadful condition. For a long time they were wedged in the window, then I concealed them in the hem of my dress. Just now I removed them from a crack in the door. It's lucky they didn't transfer me or I would have lost them all. They contain my dearest memories of her.

I am not given to crying, but when I read the letters she wrote after Helmut's death, my eyes fill with tears. I am filled with rage that she had to endure this horrible pain before she herself was executed. For security's sake, in her letters Mimi called me "Katya" or "Helenka," and she was always my dear "Roxanne." On the day before she was murdered, I got permission to visit her in her cell. I was escorted by a guard who mercifully granted my plea. Mimi had told me through the window— she was three cells away—that she was being taken to Barnimstrasse the next day. We know now what that means, going to Barnim. It's the next-to-last stop, from which the only exit is to Plotzensee. I don't think either one of us ever entertained any idle hopes . . . [fragment missing]

When we were still at the Alex, Maria learned our national anthem, which she often whistled just to cheer me up. She would summon me to the window with the first notes of this song. That evening, she whistled this melody for me for the last time—I have never heard a more beautiful rendition. With the closing bars, I broke down, sobbing in despair. That evening I wrote her my farewell letter and had hopes that I would see her one last time the next morning. The guard had promised me that, but unfortunately she couldn't keep her word. At eight o'clock,

I could hear her being taken out from her cell. They took away my most beloved child—Mimi! I didn't realize how quickly she would be taken to Plotzensee. For the next few days I tried desperately to find out whether she was still alive. For a long time they wouldn't answer my questions; finally after ten days, I was given the sad news. Though it was so painful, I was pleased that everything ended quickly, that they didn't prolong her torment. Who knows how long her nerves could have stood this terrible strain . . . [fragment missing]

Alt-Moabit, Berlin
Early September 1943

Dear Helga,

I am sure there have never been such indulged prisoners at Moabit as we are now. Life is truly splendid for us. Yesterday your Mummy ordered so much pea soup for us that all of us ended up with Buddha bellies, and we simply could not move. "Long live Sonnenschein!"

We heard today that you were bitten by an ungrateful patient.[70] Does it still hurt?

If I manage to stay alive, I will have to go to see the planetarium. Such things really interest me.

It seems that "Acetate Slime"[71] might leave us. You can imagine how upset we are about such a loss. We have only one wish—that Sonnenschein should be assigned to our section.

I'd better stop writing now or Mrs. B[auer] will tell me, once again, that I consider my work to be of secondary importance.

Thanks so much for the candies; we have never had anything so good in jail before, but do keep some for yourself, Helga.

All the best,
Your *Kleeblatt*

---

70. Helga was working in an animal hospital.
71. The hated prison guard Bauer.

Alt-Moabit, Berlin
September 18, 1943

Dearest parents,[72]

You will receive this letter after my death. It will be sent to you by a person to whom we are immeasurably indebted. She has been our friend and our guardian. At great personal risk, she tried as much as possible to ease our difficult fate; she shared with us whatever she could, never asking for anything in return. We called her our "Ray of Sunshine," because whenever she came into our cell, she brought with her joy and laughter. We became friends with her daughter. You saw her once, Daddy; do you remember?

I only regret that I will never be able to repay her for everything that she did for us, for her dear heart of gold. She was especially fond of me, and I loved her as one can only love one who offers a hand when you are truly in need and never thinks of this as charity, but only as something normal. Please don't forget her.

Dearest parents, writing this letter I still don't know what will be the outcome of my application for clemency, but believe me that I am completely ready for death, and I don't entertain any false hopes. Our long separation has deepened my feelings for you, and it pains me to leave you in such sorrow. But believe me, I am prepared to go to my death with head held high, without fear. This is my last obligation to you and to my country. Prison was for me a good, often difficult school of life, but there were nevertheless joyful, sunny days. My friendship with Mimi will remain for me an unforgettable and wonderful memory until the end. She taught me to never lose my sense of humor, to laugh at "them," and to die bravely. We will die on the eve of our victory knowing that we did not resist in vain against injustice and brute force.

Don't despair, beloved parents, and be brave, dearest Mummy. Remember that I watch over you and grieve over every one of your tears. But when you smile, I smile with you.

---

72. This letter was given to Sonnenschein, who was to keep it and forward it to the Wituski family only after Krystyna's death, which she did after the war.

May God reward you for the love and care with which you enveloped me. Farewell, dearest parents, farewell Halinka.

Your Tina

Alt-Moabit, Berlin
September 19, 1943

Dearest Mummy,

I received your letter of August 22 today. How could I possibly be angry with you? You are always my sweetest and my dearest. I told Daddy that I didn't want to see you only because I was afraid our meeting would be too hard on us, both on you and on me. After such a long time, you are sort of accustomed to my not being there, but after seeing me, it would be so hard to part again. Your nerves simply couldn't take it. And my heart would break to see your suffering and your tears. But if you get permission, do come, and show me how brave you are.

It's a sad day today. Maria is leaving us in a few hours, going to Fordon. I will miss her very much, and it's such a shame she's not going to the same place as Wanda and Olenka.

Don't be offended that I don't write long letters. But what is there to write about?

I simply can't forget about Mimi. But I am not unhappy, Mummy. Marysia will tell you some day that I was always the most cheerful one of us all.

Please thank Alina for thinking of me; she sends me such beautiful cards. They give me so much pleasure. I wanted to write to her, but it's hard for me to collect my thoughts, so I'm putting it off. Maybe I'll write later, if it's at all possible.

Please send me some stamps; I can't get them here anymore. I probably don't have to ask—no doubt you'll be sending me a box of "Camellias" and some laundry powder. And if you can send me some shampoo, then send either the one with the "little cameo" or the "oatmeal hops." The others are not very good for my hair.

Dearest little Mummy, try to keep busy all the time and never stay alone so you won't have time for unhappy thoughts; that will make it easier for you.

Heartfelt kisses, my sweetest Mummy, and give my best to everyone.

Your Tina

I need some underarm pads for my blue woolen dress and a new toothbrush.

Best wishes from Lena, the only friend I have left.

Alt-Moabit, Berlin
September 19, 1943

Dear Ursel and Gerd,

Your letters were profoundly moving. You are always expressing gratitude as though I had done heaven knows what for Maria. It was, after all, something completely natural—I loved her and wanted only the best for her. How wretched, how hopeless my life in prison would have been without her. From her I learned how to bear life with courage, and how to die. No, she didn't want you to know how desperately unhappy she was after Helmut's death. During the week I would lend her my pen so she could write her letters home. On Sundays she always felt dreadful and would say: "Our families must never know how it is here; that would only add to their anxiety; we must at least spare them that." She was very pleased that during Gerd's visit she was able to remain calm, to bear up. Seeing you that day, Gerd, brought her such joy.

I can't tell you how pleased I am with the photographs you sent. They are marvelous! Now it is easier for me to imagine Mimi's life as it once was . . . in freedom. How wonderful it must have been . . . surrounded by beauty, love, and sunshine. You don't think it's a bit much if I were to keep four photos? I just can't bear to part with them. Today is Sunday, so I am placing them all around my cell. I gaze at them constantly. There are two large photographs and two small ones. Mimi holding ears of corn, Mimi and Helmut on a knoll in the forest. When my fate is at last decided, I will definitely return these to you. It can't be much longer; it's five months today since my sentence was passed. Today my cell mate was taken away to a penal camp. We marked our separation with a feast of bread with butter and fruit that you sent us, dear Gerd.

Your letter, Ursel, expressed such love that I feel a strong attachment to you. Believe me, just as I mourned for Helmut and agonized over Mimi's pain, I now feel even more desperately your loss of Maria. Apart from Helga, I no longer have anyone anymore with whom I can share my thoughts. To my parents I write only brief, hope-filled letters. That is one thing I can't bear to think about, how terrible my death will be for them. Dear Ursel, were your worries about Mimi not enough that you are now willing to worry about me? When I write honestly, what I really feel, I'm afraid my letters cannot always be cheerful. And because of me you cannot free yourself of memories of Maria. It would be better for you to forget at last about these tragic times. No, it is neither possible nor permissible to forget, but nor is it good to think about it too much. It can drive one mad.

I hope that work will help you turn your thoughts to something else. But I, unfortunately, cannot break with them. I remain in the same cell where, only a few weeks ago, I could still hear Maria's voice. I knew her voice so well, I could always tell right away whether she was sad or in good humor.

I will probably be executed soon. But you mustn't feel sad, dear Ursel. I think that then I will see Maria again and that makes me happy.

Can you understand that sometimes death is better and easier to bear than life?

I will remember and I thank you, Ursel, that I can write to you whenever I need something. For the time being, my modest needs are looked after by my parents. One thing though: may I send my things to Halensee in the event they come for me? We can't send parcels to the Generalgouvernement, and I would like my parents to get some of my things.

I am so pleased that they sent you Maria's and Helmut's belongings. Were there some crucifixes and Madonnas among them? Mimi was furious that these lovely objects, of all things, should fall into the hands of the Gestapo.

One more thing, Gerd, when you write to my father, please tell him that everything with me is fine. Our letters take four to five weeks to get there. Can you send me some stationery and stamps? We can't buy them in prison right now. We would also like to have a map of the Russian front, preferably a newspaper clipping, though not too big, so we can hide it more easily. I thank you in advance. As for the cigarettes, they are fantastic!

I never thought that here in this alien land, and even in prison, I would find so many good friends. I am really very lucky! Sending you my very best wishes,

Your Krystyna

Dear Ursel, I would also like to have a photo of you and Gerd.

Alt-Moabit, Berlin
Sometime in September 1943

[To Helga,]

Despite this being one of the tenets of National Socialism, I do think that women should marry and have children because I believe that way our lives will be fulfilled. But why would you have to leave your profession to marry? It seems to me that one can't be so limited; a woman who has nothing besides home and children and wants to know nothing else is as uninteresting as one who understands nothing of family life.

I was absolutely amazed to read in the *Volkischer Beobachter* today this article: "The trio of traitors fled to Palermo and gave themselves up to the protection of the Allies." Of course they are talking about the king [of Italy], the heir to the throne, and Marshall Badoglio. Ach, how

I envy those lucky people. No, I take that back. They are contemptible![73]

Alt-Moabit, Berlin
September 24, 1943

Dear Teddy,[74]

How's your hand? Are you able to write yet? I just got my first letter from Ursel, just as I had given up hope of its getting through. As affectionate as ever. I almost envy you, that tomorrow you'll be able to meet her.

Teddy, Can you fix my pen? I have endless problems with it. It would be such a shame if I couldn't use it anymore. I got it from a good friend who is probably not alive anymore.[75] I've managed to hang on to it through all my interrogations, trials, and prisons, and in the end, it's the one Mimi used to write her final letter. You can imagine how I treasure it. It will be yours, when I'm gone.

Teddy, I'm forwarding to you some letters from my friend and neighbor, Jutta. We spent six months together in this section. She expected a death sentence, but—Praise God!—she got eight years in prison. She was taken to Cottbus last week. She's a twenty-five-year-old woman who has a little daughter. What a splendid companion she was!

I must tell you something. Last night, there was an alarm. Sonnenschein was on duty, and she came to us. I stood beside her at the door. She caressed my face, and then I held her hand so tightly. I can't explain how I felt, as though I were with my own mother—a feeling of security as I haven't had for a long time. For a moment I did not feel like an orphan. Are you angry that I stole your mother for this moment?

Teddy! Sonnenschein is here and I am writing these words using the

---

73. Italy had been Germany's ally but surrendered following the Allied invasion.
74. To Helga, but from now on, for safety's sake, addressed to a boy, "Teddy."
75. Karol Szapiro. She must have received word that he was missing again.

pencil you gave me. How can I thank you enough for your presents, for your long letter, and especially for going to visit Gerd so promptly. I am so sorry that he suffered so much on my account.[76]

The Dragon did that on purpose. We will now forget all about that and live as "carefree" as before. Poor Gerd sent me what is almost a fare-well letter. I'm sure you'll remember to call him and explain everything, tell him I'm still alive, and I was delighted to get the cigarettes. I can't smoke them right now, it's still too early, but oh, how lovely they smell. I think the song is lovely, but I wish I knew the melody. You may keep the photographs as long as you like; I don't need them. I am very worried about the bad news from the eastern front. Do you think it would be possible to hold the Bolsheviks at the Dnieper for long? It would be a vile, dirty trick to kill us now, don't you think? If the Dragon had been "lucky," I would now be shorter by a head! That thought does not spoil my appetite, and I am terribly hungry right now. I hope that soon we will have supper, with pears from Gerd! Then I will use those horrible black dresses that I have to sew to make a comfortable spot for myself where I will sit and smoke a cigarette. Now I ask you, who could ask for anything more? Loads of good wishes and a big kiss from,

Your grateful Kryscha.[77]

Alt-Moabit, Berlin[78]
Sometime in September 1943

What luck that you did this, otherwise I'd have been in a fatal mess. I keep reading your letter and Gerd's over and over again; I keep looking at Mimi's photograph, slowly sucking a candy all the while, and I just

---

76. Gerd Terwiel thought that Krystyna had been executed after hearing from the hated guard, "the Dragon," that one of two Polish girls was going to Plotzensee for execution.

77. The diminutive of the name Krystyna is Krysia, here, however, spelled the German way.

78. Fragment of letter smuggled to Helga.

can't believe that all this is for real. Thank you, Teddy, for describing everything to me in such detail, but oh, how I envy you!!!!! Will I ever be able to look at Mimi's picture again, listen to her records of her favorite songs? Please, please write to me everything to the finest detail so that I can imagine that I was actually there. I am so pleased that you are willing to go see him again. So, I will have another letter ready for Friday. It was really nice of you to remember that little poem.

Do you really think that this won't last much longer??? After supper, I pasted the newspaper to the wall with the headline "Badoglio's Cowardly Treason" so I could feast my eyes on it.

Dear, good God, don't let me die now—when everything is turning out well. I could weep from sorrow that Mimi did not live long enough to see this. She would be delirious with joy!!!

How I hate to have to part with your and Gerd's letters today. Teddy, I am so terribly agitated, I can hardly write. Tell me, how can I thank you? Meanwhile, I am sending you a big fat kiss and lots and lots of good wishes.

Your Krysia

Alt-Moabit, Berlin[79]
September 1943

[First part missing]. . . I often used to write home about Mimi and her brother and sister. You must ask Gerd if they received Mimi's farewell letters. I know she wrote them a week before her death. Surely they wouldn't be so cruel as to censor those. That I wouldn't understand!!! Among Mimi's papers there was a small photograph that I once gave her. So now the situation is that I don't have any photos here with me; they are in a suitcase in a storage closet. Tomorrow I will try to go upstairs and steal them. I have a feeling I'll succeed because, as you know, I am by now quite skilled at this sort of thing. I think your photography plans are fantastic! No doubt you will be as determined in this as in

---

79. Fragment of letter to Helga.

everything else. As for the business of the newspaper, I must humbly confess that I only got daring enough to hang it up once I knew that no one other than Sonnenschein would be around.

You know, Teddy, when Mimi and I were at the Alex, we used to spin stories for hours on end about a magic ring that could make us invisible. Then, with the big stick that was used for opening the ventilators, we killed our horrible guards and policemen, rescued Helmut, and then all the political prisoners from all the jails and camps. Our storytelling would practically make us feverish, and Mimi would say, "Wouldn't that be wonderful, Kryscha, oh so wonderful!"

Teddy, we agree about your name and know exactly how to use it. I like it. But we still have to decide how we are going to write "Krysia." Should it be the Polish way, "Krysia," or the way Mimi wrote it, "Kryscha"? She pronounced it so nicely. Germans can't quite pronounce our "sia." So let's keep on using "Kryscha" in memory of Mimi. Dear little *Bazyliszek,*[80] I wish you good luck in your work, and I must finish now or I doubt I will manage to write today to my poor parents. Love and best wishes,

Your Kryscha

Alt-Moabit, Berlin
September 1943

Dear Teddy,

Well, today I had no luck. That witch never took her eyes off me, so I couldn't get at my stuff in the storage closet. But I just had to have it [Mimi's photograph], so I did something I rarely and reluctantly do—I asked—and on the spot I invented a sad story about my fiancé and how much I would like to send him my photo as a last memento. That woman's heart must be made of stone. She just yelled at me. But Krystyna does not give up so easily! I have already registered a request to talk with the supervisor, and I will tell her the same sad tale. I am hop-

---

80. A little dragon, used affectionately here.

ing for favorable results, but if not, then I will have to hope for better luck and try again to steal them out of storage.

Yesterday we got letters from home that were in transit for over a month, and I also got one from my fiancé. I must now explain this matter to you. I haven't seen this boy in five years; I went off to Switzerland for a year immediately after our engagement. I returned to Poland just a few weeks before war broke out. I didn't see him, because he had already been mobilized. He was taken prisoner. Do you know where we finally met after almost four years separation? Here in Berlin, during an interrogation by the Gestapo. Funny, isn't it? I was caught simply because they found my address in his papers, but, in fact, our two cases were not at all related. I have no feelings for him and wouldn't marry him if I survived. But I wouldn't break our engagement now, I wouldn't do this to him at a time like this; besides, there is no need to since I will soon be dead. He is still so young. I feel that I am much more mature; I feel sorry for him that he must spend so many years a captive away from his country. He is, all in all, a brave and very decent boy. But really, I'm far from being in love with him.

Your letter arrived and I've read it; the best moment of the day is past. I was struck speechless when I saw the grapes, I am still . . . [next page missing]

Alt-Moabit, Berlin
September 30, 1943

Dear Gerd,

Oh, happy day—your eagerly awaited letter arrived. I just can't imagine life without mail from Halensee.

Thank you so much for those delicious things; these are not trifles you send us, dear Gerd. We know that there are shortages in town, so we appreciate it all the more! I would happily starve and freeze if I thought that would make the war end more quickly. I was amused to hear that you find writing letters in German difficult. I suspect that these difficulties arise from the fact that you don't know me very well yet. Every word from you is all the dearer as I know from Maria that you are very reserved.

Wouldn't it be wonderful if some day I could move from Moabit to Halensee. We used to make such plans with Maria, and it is really so nice that you had the same idea. What would I do in that strange, foreign town?

Ah, Gerd, if the right moment comes, you will take me from here, right? If Maria and I had only had a file, we would have cut through the grate and escaped; we were constantly plotting this, but we never had an opportunity . . . [fragment missing]

I often wrote to my mother about Maria. She was to pray for her just as much as she prayed for me, especially since Maria's mother knew nothing about this whole tragedy.

The guard that gave us such a scare last week was just here. She wanted to say good-bye since she is leaving permanently. She even wanted to shake hands—what a strange person! But I forgave her everything because she took me to see Mimi that last evening.

Dear Gerd, Ursel offered to send me some lingerie, but is it not too forward of me to ask for such things? Nights are awfully cold here, and a warm nightdress or a warm jacket would be most useful.

It's getting dark so I must finish now. My luxurious cigarette hour is approaching, and I will continue thinking of you.

All the best from me and from little Lena.

Your Krystyna W.

Alt-Moabit, Berlin
September 30, 1943

Dear Teddy,

Thanks so much for fixing my pen and for the notepad. Would it be too nervy to ask you for something else? It's been a long time since we got any parcels from home. I need some cotton wool since I haven't received any sanitary packages from home in a long time.

The tablets have helped me a lot on two occasions.

You didn't write me a word about Ursel. We are very pleased that your hands are all better. Was the movie good? One more kiss from your K.

When will you go see Gerd again?

I had a nightmare about Mimi today. I had to watch her suffer, and I was not able to help her. I woke up sobbing terribly.

Alt-Moabit, Berlin
Early October 1943

Forgive me for writing on such a card. You are going to have a lot of problems with my letters if you really want to preserve them all. Could you mention to Ursel or Gerd that little Lena needs a pad of writing paper, and I some headache tablets. Is it still possible to buy a notebook in Berlin? I must go now and read *V.B.* [the newspaper *Volkischer Beobachter*]. Well, dear Teddy, get well soon.

All the best,
Your Kryscha

Alt-Moabit, Berlin
Early October 1943

Dear Teddy,

The Lice Patrol has organized a lice hunt. The stench is horrible. They are trying to gas us!

Section Four is so lucky; Sonnenschein is on duty there today. But we have seen her today and read your letter. Lena received a lot of mail from home today. Her sister has spoken to my mother, who lives in a state of deep sorrow because she also gets no mail from me. Maybe she thinks I am already dead? Listen, Teddy, could you send her an anonymous letter? Just one sentence: "Krystyna is well and getting along fine." That would mean so much to her; you would spare her lots of tears and sleepless nights. You are so dear, Teddy, I have to love you more and more each day. I'm delighted with the beautiful poems. Of course I need some "Camellia" pads, but cotton wool would also be appreciated if only it's not too difficult for Sonnenschein to smuggle it in.

Dinner soon. Wonder what slop we'll get.

With a bellyful of potato soup, I now continue this letter. Isn't it disgusting that they force us to work? At least the people condemned to death could be spared this! Instead of that boring work making buttonholes, I would rather study or read. Our neighbor will receive her sentence today, probably death. I am afraid she might not be strong enough morally to take this bravely. I wish her luck. I feel sorry for them, no matter who they are.

I am as pleased as you are that you can travel with the woman doctor.[81]

Kisses from your K.

Alt-Moabit, Berlin
October 3, 1943

My dear Teddy,

I am sorry that you once again went to bed so late because of me. I must thank you for your letter, for all our presents, and your help. Above all for those stolen American cigarettes. You are right, Teddy, my idea about the parcels wasn't well thought out. I myself didn't have much hope that Gerd would forward the card. But you see, Teddy, it would give me such pleasure if I could at least once pay you back for all that you do for me. We laughed our heads off over Gerd's boxer shorts. Mimi got the same kind of shorts from home when we were at the Alex, and every morning and evening, when she put them on, I would laugh myself sick.

I strongly protest against certain secrets between Lena and Gerd! I know that when Lena asks for something for me, she does so with the

---

81. Details not known.

best intentions, but I know best what I need, and I don't want to load Gerd down with all these requests.

We are so lucky today because Sonnenschein is here. She managed to get us an iron, and we had something to do all morning.

Forgive me, Teddy, but I can't write about anything else today. I am sick with hate and revenge! Our neighbor did get the death sentence, of course, and tomorrow is going to Barnim(strasse). She is brave and serene, she won't shame us—the political prisoners. Last night I couldn't sleep thinking about all the Nazi war crimes. Innumerable crimes and murders. Teddy, what you have seen here is child's play compared to the atrocities they commit in Poland. Yesterday Betty asked me why Germans hate us so much, and consider us "subhuman." This is all their propaganda because they want to take over our country for themselves by wiping out all Polish leadership. They want to justify their bloody deeds. I don't understand why they brought me here to Berlin and proceeded to play out this comedy with the military court. In Warsaw, they simply take two pistol shots, right on the street, to kill somebody. The Gestapo does not bother with ceremony with the Poles. When they took me from my home at night, I figured I had, at the most, a couple of days to live. I had no idea what they knew about me.

My God, if they knew everything, they would have killed me at once! My poor mother was scared to death when I said good-bye to her. I hugged her for the last time and managed to whisper in her ear, "Be brave and pray for me." I knew right then that this was my final farewell.

Now I know why I am here. The officers and gentlemen here must have something to do so they won't be sent to the front. What very important and hard work it is to condemn all these young girls to death! You know, it amazes me how righteously they carry out their propaganda about the mass graves at Katyn.[82] Their own methods, after all,

---

82. The site of a mass grave found in the USSR. The Soviets murdered over 15,000 POWs, officers of the Polish army, who were captured when the Soviets invaded Poland in 1939. Despite Germany's propaganda, the Soviets denied their guilt, accusing the Nazis of the crime. It was not until 1992 that Boris Yeltsin finally officially admitted Soviet guilt and delivered to Poland the documents ordering the executions, bearing Stalin's signature.

are identical. They can "organize" such things very well; in the space of two, three months, they emptied the entire Warsaw Ghetto. There were over 600,000 people there. Men, women, children. Nobody came out alive. They transported the Jews to two great camps in the east part of the Generalgouvernement. There they were put to death in gas chambers. If you go past these camps in a train, you can smell the burning bodies. People close the windows and hold their noses. These are not fairy tales, Teddy, I was there. I saw it, I lived through it. Starving Jewish children, trying to escape from the ghetto, thrown like kittens into the gutters. People shot in the streets like dogs or deported to Germany as slaves. Whenever I was late coming home, my mother trembled with anxiety that I would never return. All Warsaw mothers tremble so for their children—if they still have them—because Polish youth is being tortured to death, killed in prisons and concentration camps. I told you once, Teddy, that the Polish nation is a peaceful one, but you shouldn't be surprised if they are now sharpening their knives and thinking about revenge.

They hate everything German like the plague because they don't see any decent Germans, only tyrants, murderers, torturers. And this gang of murderers knows too well that if they are defeated, there will be no forgiving. They will try to kill us all because they would fear the survivors. I became a person eager for revenge; I consider it essential to avenge humanity, to finally exterminate that vermin. Can you understand this, Teddy? I curse with fury the Soviet-German pact.[83] Damn them! There, that eases my anger.

Which of Schiller's poems do you want to send me? I have read many of them, and my favorite is "Don Carlos." I also had one of Uhland's books once.

We just got our dinner. Sonnenschein gave us lots of pea soup. I tell you, Teddy, a full belly is terrible torture; I must sit very erect and move very slowly. But here, my neighbors don't give me any peace—every five minutes I climb up on my sewing machine. They keep calling: "Krys-

---

83. The Molotov-Ribbentrop Pact, signed in August 1939, formalized Soviet-German collaboration in the attack and partition of Poland, defining their respective occupation zones and cooperation in suppressing resistance.

cha. Kryscha." Only once I really jumped when I heard, "The army is retreating from Naples." That changed my mood!

Can you imagine, today there was no other guard around besides Sonnenschein. That is really wonderful.

Will we spend Christmas here? I doubt it. More to the point, will we still be alive a week from now? I don't want to lose hope . . . hope . . . hope.

Well, I took advantage of an occasion to get hold of a newspaper, so I will end this letter now. Anyway, Sonnenschein will soon come to pick it up.

Best wishes, hugs, and kisses to my dear little Teddy,
Your Kryscha

Many thanks for the eraser. I want to draw something for your *Kleeblatt* album. I don't know how successful I'll be though; I have absolutely no artistic talent.

You must draw something like this for your *Kleeblatt* album: a white eagle on a red background and these three words, which mean: God—Honor—Country. That would immediately signify that we are Polish and we were fighting for our country.

Alt-Moabit, Berlin
October 5, 1943

Dear Teddy,

I feel strange. Sometimes I ask myself, do I still think and feel like a normal person, or like a madwoman? My thoughts and memories torment me. But how can I keep my mind occupied when I have to sew those cursed buttonholes all day? Ahh, if I could only stop thinking. Oh, how I miss my home. For months I didn't experience this feeling. Everything seemed so remote, as though it were just a dream, but suddenly it is again upon me, and it hurts so much. What a weakling I am to be writing to you about this when I know so well that nobody can help me if I can't find strength within myself. We must learn to rely on ourselves. This is all egotism; I think too much about myself. When Mimi was still here, I didn't have time for that and I felt much better.

[Fragment missing]

Alt-Moabit, Berlin
October 6, 1943

My dear Teddy,

I am so ashamed of all my complaining in yesterday's letter, but yesterday was exactly two months since Mimi's death.

We've been told that you're sick; we're very concerned and feel very sorry for our poor little Teddy. I can never thank you enough for writing to my mother. You wrote exactly what I wished you would write.

I'm really sorry about this, Teddy, but I must once again criticize your countrymen and defend my own. Believe me, I really see things as they are, and I am not influenced by my own particular situation. I am not that limited in my outlook. Nor will I ever go so far as to hate an entire nation.

Much was exaggerated in the news reports here about the war in Poland. You know what propaganda is all about. It's true that quite a few *Volksdeutschen* [ethnic Germans] were killed in Bydgoszcz. The murderers were ordinary criminals who had been released from prison when the war started. This killing was to avenge the Polish soldiers who were machine-gunned by *Volksdeutsche* civilians. Such bloody events are part of the history of all wars once criminals are let loose. I was living in Wartheland, a region with many German communities and no harm came to them, nor in Łódź for that matter, where there were very many Germans. Do you know any German whose relatives were killed during "Bloody Sunday" in Bydgoszcz?[84] I doubt it. I certainly don't. On the other hand, I don't know a single Polish family that hasn't lost a son or a father at German hands. What the Germans are doing to the Jews, and to us, is nothing other than cold-blooded genocide. It is guided by the

---

84. A city in Poland, the site of heavy fighting in the early months of the war.

ruthless politics of National Socialism directed against those who are weaker but who will not submit. Why did they send all the priests from Wartheland to concentration camps and close all the churches? They also closed the schools in Wartheland and deprived all Polish children of an education. All Polish leadership was destroyed, Polish farmers and workers are not permitted to study, but are forced to work mindlessly for their new overlords. In Warsaw, they have liquidated half of all lawyers, university professors, doctors, writers, and other professionals. There is not a single secondary school left open. Anyone who wants to continue her education must do so underground, but this is costly. Germans are particularly cruel in Warsaw because they know that it is there that they will never extinguish the flame of resistance, that there lies the center of all underground organizations. There, the fight for freedom continues ceaselessly, day and night . . . [end missing]

Alt-Moabit, Berlin
October 7, 1943

Dear Teddy,

Just a few words to send my regards to my dear Teddy Bear. I am, at this moment, devouring the most delicious honey cake and overflowing with gratitude to S.s.[85] I even got two cigarettes!!!

Today I also received some mail from home that was mailed very long ago. I got a letter from my sister; what an unexpected honor!!! The only thing in the whole world that interests my sister is her little son. She is blind and deaf to everything else. Pity you can't read this letter!!! It is an ode in praise of her child's intelligence (he's a year old) and there's not a single word of feeling toward me. What an odd woman!

Lena sends many thanks for your letter. Unfortunately, she doesn't have time right now to reply.

---

85. From here on, Sonnenschein is usually abbreviated as S.s.

I must finish now because S.s. will soon be here, though I would like to gab a little longer with you.

Best wishes and kisses,

Your K.

Alt-Moabit, Berlin
October 8, 1943

Addressed to *An Herrn Teddy-Bar*

Dear Teddy,

I feel I must send you at least a few words. I can't manage anything longer right now, perhaps this evening. They seem to think that I have turned into an electric machine, and each day they demand more work. Did the light help?[86] I got another letter from my mother today. Conditions in Warsaw are getting worse all the time. Bandits cruise the streets in their cars, enter any home that appeals to them, and take what they want. The villages are terrorized by bandits. Starvation is as common as in India since the Germans have requisitioned everything for themselves. Bringing food into Warsaw from the countryside is strictly forbidden. *My beloved, old Warsaw—how I would love to see you again!* [87]

We feel quite well. Lena has been terribly busy all day????[88] And I am furious because my newspaper carrier did not show up when I went out for my walk. I finish now with a big kiss and lots of good wishes.

Your Kryscha

---

86. Possibly referring to photography. Helga had recently bought herself a camera.

87. This last sentence was written in Polish even though the letter to Helga is in German.

88. The significance of the question marks is not clear.

Alt-Moabit, Berlin
October 9, 1943

Dear Teddy,

My stomach still hurts from laughing so hard. Have some consideration for us and don't write so many hilarious things all at once or you'll finish us off. We are delighted that you liked the slippers. Lena knitted a pair just like yours for me too.

Thanks so much for the poems. I especially like the serious ones; they suit my mood, and so my favorite is "Die Nachtreise und auf der Winterreise."

I've been toying with a new idea ever since S.s. told me that all the guards are taking shooting lessons. Does that mean that they will soon be carrying guns? If so, I have a great plan ready. When one of them comes here in the evening, we will drag her into the cell, bind her mouth with one of the blouses, wrap her head in some of the woolen dresses, tie her hands tight behind her back, and put her on the floor in the corner covered with our blankets and pallets. We will capture her pistol and her keys, and so armed, will exit our cells. (N.B. We must remember to take a piece of sausage with us because, according to Lena, there are some vicious dogs in the courtyard. We can save a little of the sausage from our Sunday supper.) We shall march out to the exit, and Lena will open the doors while I will stand guard with pistol ready. The men at the door will be astonished, but they will just have to hold their arms up or else they'll get a bullet in the leg. We'll run to the gate and, like gazelles, leap over it and disappear into the night. No, you'll never be able to understand this!

Lena says we must do a practice run. Great, but on whom? There's S.s., but we can't be brutal with her. Ah, Teddy, when I think these things I have to tell you: It would be so wonderful to enjoy freedom once again. I didn't go for my walk today; I just can't stand the insulting abuse and the horrid faces of those witches.

Ach, you know, if my plan with the guns did not work and I couldn't escape, I could at least kill a few Nazis and finally shoot myself in the head. That would be preferable than to be led like a sheep to my execution. Don't you think so?

Tomorrow I will read, and I will write a longer letter to my mother. I have finished the book about the Volga Germans; it was excellent.

You misunderstood me. I wrote that I am tired by the thoughts whirling in my head and not by being unable to think. It is precisely this incessant thinking about the same things that wears me out. I wish it were possible to somehow suspend all thinking, the way one does when asleep. But all of this is unimportant; the most important—that they would let us live! My fiancé's mother wrote me that her son's lawyer told her my situation is mildly improved.

Best regards from Julianna,[89]
Your Kryscha

Alt-Moabit, Berlin
October 12, 1943

My dear Teddy,

We just finished reading your long letter. What a coincidence, I was also thinking of you on Sunday, and I made you a little doll dressed in a Polish folk costume. I went to a lot of trouble trying to overcome my lethargy. Do you like it? To get the material for it, we made two dresses 5 cm shorter. The face and hands are made out of one of my slips. (Don't worry, I have another.) I wouldn't want a home in the forest, it's too cold now—or maybe we could sleep in Uncle Tom's Cabin? That would be fantastic! Especially, of course, in the evening!

Reading your story, before dinner, about the venison and gravy, I got furious, but now I can take it calmly, even if you were to write about a roast goose. S.s. saved us from hunger once again. In fact we still have a full bowl of soup, and Lena is trying to figure out how to keep it warm. I suggested that she put the sewing machine light into the bowl, or she could sit on the bowl, but she doesn't listen to me. The cake was fabulous!!!!!!!!

---

89. Perhaps alluding to the little rag doll—later referred to as Julia—that Krystyna made for Helga.

We have been thinking for some time, along with Betty and Tanka from cell #20, about making a film about prison life: "The Battle of the Maidens." A worthwhile project.

"Die Burgschaft"—absolutely beautiful. Thank you so much for going to all the trouble of copying such a long piece for me. You know, I read this once, but returning to it is all the more pleasant. I also loved the poem about autumn. I can hardly wait to see what Gerd has found for me.

Our thoughts will be with you this evening, my Teddy. I hope you will have less pain. We were so delighted to see your photos. I always think of you as an adult, so I am amazed to see before me a teenager—where do you keep all those serious thoughts?

Tomorrow is Wednesday, but surely nothing will happen to us the day before you go to see Gerd.

Yesterday I had such pain in my stomach that I kept holding the sewing machine lamp against me all day. Ever since I've been in prison, I feel awful when I am menstruating. The tablets you sent me help. I must go now because those damn buttonholes are waiting. Hope you feel better soon.

Best wishes and kisses,
Your Kryscha

How nice of you to think of Marysia. I'm sure she'll hold out. Poland needs such women! I'm sure she's always thinking of us and longs for news.

Alt-Moabit, Berlin
October 14, 1943

Dear Teddy Bear,

Did you go the doctor's yesterday? I was thinking of you again. I'm worried about Lena. She's had a bad cold for a week, and she's so unreasonable. But there's nothing I can do. She gets offended if I suggest something and, like a child, says that her cold doesn't disturb anybody.

I'm glad you like the doll. I want to make another one for S.s., but I don't have any wool for the hair. Do you have some at home?

Wednesday is over, thank God. I'm so glad you went to Halensee.[90] I am reading a terrific book; I'm absolutely captivated by it. It's the first part of *Im Wolga Land,* titled *Die Vater zogen aus.* I learned quite a few interesting things. There's a marvelous account of a pilgrimage to Aachen. Now I'm reading about the court of Catherine II in Petersburg.

You know, I rather doubt that the war will end this year. It infuriates me that the Germans are such good soldiers. How they do this—that is a mystery to me?! I must give them credit, but I would love to see them retreating!

How awful it will be when the Russians enter Poland. And yet I wish for this, because this curse from the east is the only way out.[91]

Lena has gone for her walk; I stayed in the cell. I can hear the water in the pipes; when I close my eyes, I imagine that I am sitting at a river's edge. Ah, if I only knew what plans they have for me. October 19 will be exactly one year since my arrest and exactly six months since I was sentenced to death. It's enough to drive a person mad. I'm closing now and waiting for S.s.

Best wishes and a big, fat kiss—my dear, little Teddy.

Your Kryscha

S.s. was just here; she quickly deposited a package for us and disappeared. The honey cake disappeared almost as quickly into our empty stomachs. If it weren't for that marvelous taste still lingering in our mouths, I would think the cake was just a dream. I want to send Ursel's letter through you rather than the official way; the censors would delay it and it wouldn't reach Karlsbrunn until about mid-November. The gentlemen of the RKG [*Reichskriegsgericht:* the Reich War Court] don't rush these things. I think I'll send Marysia a card tomorrow. The worst that can happen is that it will be returned to me. Enjoyed your letter.

---

90. Home of Mimi's brother Gerd.

91. Since the Soviet Union, in collaboration with Germany, occupied Poland from September 1939 until June 1941, the Poles quite realistically dreaded the suffering and death that a Soviet "liberation" would bring.

Alt-Moabit, Berlin
October 14, 1943

My dear Teddy,

Cigarettes—from you? What a surprise! You are an angel; no, more than that—you are an archangel, and I send you lots and lots of kisses and a million thanks. Lena bemoans the fact that she is not a smoker, but I can't make this decision for her; I have been considering whether I should give her my portion of the cake in compensation, but that is not a decision I would make in haste. I am so sorry I missed little Julia Hulajnóżka's baptism. In fact, I could have officiated. I am confident that your child will not bring you any sorrows, only joy.

I must finish, Teddy, because I'm afraid of being caught by that horrible Bauer. She was very polite to me today. "Don't look so sour, Krystyna!" she said. What nerve!!! (Did I spell *dores Gesich* correctly?)

Once again, thanks for everything.

Until the next time,

Your Kryscha

Alt-Moabit, Berlin
October 15, 1943

My dear Teddy,

I am delirious with excitement! Isn't that girl's escape the most amazing feat?[92] She's been telling us all along that she intends to try this, but we never took it seriously. We just saw her on Monday at the garment stockroom and spoke to her quite a bit. She was to be executed on Wednesday. She waited until the last minute because she was afraid her escape might affect her sister's situation. Her sister was in the same cell with her. But the last night that she was still here in Moabit, she told us she would escape. She was so tiny, so slender, that she could squeeze through the grate; she had actually tried it a couple of times. But how

---

92. Stefania Przybył, a fellow prisoner.

did she get down from the third floor? Incredible! She did it during an air raid alarm, then crossed over to the second courtyard where she either mixed in with the people coming out of the air-raid shelters, or she waited until five o'clock in the morning when the gate is open. She could observe all the movements from her window. Super girl! You can't imagine how I envy her.

She lived here in Berlin and had obtained the status of *Reichsdeutsch*,[93] but she remained loyal to Poland and worked in a Polish espionage organization. She was in the same conspiracy as Marta Rachel, who is in a nearby cell. Marta is also condemned to death. No doubt they will soon deal with her sister, since they were put together the last few days before Stefania was to be executed. How awful she must have felt that she could not escape with her! But at least one got away from the clutches of those bloodthirsty Nazis. We expect there'll be some new security regulations.

Teddy, isn't it awful that my head is too big? I think the grate on the upper floors is wider. That damned grate! Beneath my window is a wall surrounding a courtyard, so I could easily then jump to another yard where civilians live so there's sure to be an exit to a street. I shiver just thinking about it. I hope they don't capture this girl!!!

All the best and lots of kisses, dear Teddy,
Your Kryscha

Alt-Moabit, Berlin
October 17, 1943

Dear Gerd,

Another lucky week has passed. Almost every week someone goes to Plotzensee and every Tuesday I think: well, Wednesday is the day . . . I aver it is better to be prepared for everything rather than be shocked by the unexpected. On Wednesday, when the danger is past, our joy is all the greater because we were expecting . . .

---

93. Some Poles of German origin were offered the status of German citizenship.

I want to express my most heartfelt thanks for the apples and the cigarettes. I am only sorry that I am stealing from your already small store of cigarettes. You are no doubt accustomed to smoking while I, for a long time now, have grown accustomed to doing without.

Lena and I were truly touched that you will send us some of your own underwear. We also think it is very funny. I can just see the shocked expression on the head guard (an old maid) when, during an inspection, she pulls it out of my bundle. I will tell her a story about my dear, thoughtful brother; I just hope I will be able to keep a straight face.

The hymn to Mary was very beautiful. Our light is on until eight these days. After supper, we arrange our cell as cozily as possible, and then we read and write. These are the best hours of the day, when we are left alone. Nobody bothers us, we don't have to look at their twisted faces or listen to their detestable voices. Heavenly peace!

But I don't want silence! I want out of these four walls, this entrapment is a contradiction of life!

From time to time, just as I think that everything inside me has died, I am once again overtaken by a wild longing.

Please give my best to Ursel, I will write to her as well.

And all the best to you today from,

Krystyna

Alt-Moabit, Berlin
October 17, 1943

Dear Teddy,

We are in good spirits, we will not be subdued!! They put us in chains now at night!!! Bastards!!!

Tell S.s. not to cry so much. We love her so much, her tears. . . .

Kisses,

Kryscha

October 17, 1943

My dear Teddy, I shall continue. Maybe S.s. will come here again today. What I wanted to tell you was that we can't bear to see her crying. We have resigned ourselves to our fate [the chains]; it wasn't easy and I cursed mightily—and that got it out of my system. The first night was terrible; we hardly slept, but last night we were so exhausted that we fell asleep quite quickly. The handcuffs are old and heavy; they must be from the eighteenth century, and they're very painful on the wrists. I suppose that in time I will get used to this humiliation. Ach, Teddy, you could die laughing watching me pull Lena's pants down when she has to pee. The worst part is that one of us has to go to sleep quite uncovered since it's impossible to cover oneself. I could use a warm jacket and some warm underwear because I gave away my woolen things.

Now that we have such a distinguished neighbor, we don't dare carry on conversations through the windows.[94]

Ah, Teddy, things were pretty grim for a while because we were sure we'd be sent to Barnim[strasse]. It would be awful to part with S.s., with you, Ursel and Gerd, and then a new jail again. Better to go straight to Plotzensee!!! We are glad we can remain here. All our guards behave decently toward us and even Miss Bauer was somehow different when she came to put us in our chains last night.

Everything passes; every night of torment is followed by sunshine— today I got a letter from my beloved mother. And Gerd's letter gave me such pleasure.

So long as S.s. is with us, everything is bearable. Best wishes and heartfelt kisses to you, my dear, kind Teddy,

Your Kryscha

Little Lena is so lovable and brave. Yesterday she again fell from the window and hurt herself quite badly. Poor little thing.

---

94. A night supervisor was assigned to the floor after Stefania's escape.

Alt-Moabit, Berlin
October 1943

Dear Teddy,

As you can imagine, I was so emotional on Friday night, I couldn't sleep. Now I must write to Gerd. I regret now that I destroyed so many of Mimi's letters; but I'm really pleased with my luck in at least saving the rest.

Will Sonnenschein be bringing us another letter from you? We sure hope so!!! I'm very embarrassed because I think I forgot to thank you for the delicious chocolates.

Teddy, from now on when we write about political matters, let's play a game of opposites, that is, we'll write the opposite of what we mean. Mimi and I used to do that. For example:

Poor, poor Duce [Mussolini], when I read that those gangsters carted him on a stretcher, shackled in chains, and loaded him into a van, I cried so much that the newspaper was drenched with my tears. The last newspaper was so tragic and so interesting that I read it aloud to the girls. It depressed us so much. Once the Americans come up against our armies in Italy, then, when we're bombed, I suppose we'll have to go—of our own free will—to the cellars for safety.

It's a shame that Marysia and Lena are not inclined to be enthusiastic. I wish Mimi were still here. She would be cheering like mad. I get so mad when I think about the Dragon getting yet another victim. I am tough, skinny, and not easily digestible. My neighbor from #17 is less sensible than I am—she tried to out-shout the Dragon. It was a real circus; even the supervisor came downstairs. The poor thing realized that the enemy had a distinct advantage and was forced to capitulate.

Today was Sunday and we should have gone to chapel, but we didn't. A new edict has been issued—foreigners are forbidden to go to church. If we can't, we can't; God won't abandon us just because of that. The Führer himself expressed the opinion that the Almighty will bestow a military cross and a laurel wreath on those nations that, in the hour of their most trying afflictions and most bitter adversity, will not forget their duty to maintain their national honor. So we can be quite sure of ourselves!

Teddy, you have no idea how much it pleased me to learn that you too are capable of great love and admiration for certain people. You know, one friend is all I need, and for that friend I would sacrifice anything, even my life. And everything I would do for this friend would be a pleasure and not an obligation. I must admit that because of this I have suffered a lot. But that doesn't matter; the important thing is that my life is not meaningless and empty like that of people who are only tepid and never passionate.

Teddy, I have a request: If the war should end, or if there's a revolution, would you and Sonnenschein please remember to get me out of prison? I hope I will still be alive when that happens. You know, I wouldn't want to be transported back to Poland along with everybody else. I want to look around Berlin first. What an optimist! Oh, here's Sonnenschein with your letter. Dear Teddy, I am frequently overwhelmed by your feelings about everything that concerns Mimi and me. Don't be afraid that the letter and photographs made me sad—it would be a lie to deny it—because at the same time, I was happy that I could tell Mimi's family about everything. I'm sure that Mimi would be very pleased with us. By all means show the letter to Gerd—that will spare me having to write it again for him. And of course you can give him my father's address (just don't confuse it with my mother's address in Warsaw):

Feliks Wituski, Poczta Brwinow, Majątek Brwinow, Generalgouvernement.

Alt-Moabit, Berlin
October 1943

My dear Teddy,

Thanks so much for your letter. We are stitching handbags now—it's utterly depressing. We rarely get out now for a walk—the five of us who are condemned to death, that is. They have taken away all our things though we managed to hang on to our slacks and stockings. Every evening they take away everything including our clothes. At times, we find it all quite funny. Last night, while they were putting on our chains, we had a visit from our distinguished neighbor, who inquired whether we were able to sleep. "Yes, yes," she said, "I'm next door and I too can't sleep" (for fear that one of us might escape, no doubt).

Tanka is so small and sweet. They both speak such funny German; I suspect that soon I too will speak that way since I hear this funny language all the time. I'm so lucky. I got a book of Goethe's poems from the prison library. They're absolutely beautiful!

Ah, you know Teddy, Sonnenschein is so lovable, and all the prisoners are so thoughtful, that we don't feel abandoned and we wear our chains—as you said—with pride. Dear Teddy Bear, thinking of you and your sweet letters helps us so much. They let me keep Mimi's big photo, so I will have her always by my side. When you get a chance, tell Gerd that Lena and I send our best regards. Many thanks for the cigarettes; although I can't smoke them, I nevertheless appreciate your thoughtfulness.

Best wishes and kisses from your poor, exhausted, but still smiling *Kleeblatt.*

Alt-Moabit, Berlin
October 1943

[First part missing]

I was discussing my love for Mimi with Marysia. She asked me whether it is worthwhile devoting so much attention to just one person; would it not be more profitable to preserve one's passion for greater things. Perhaps she thinks I am exaggerating, though she didn't say so. But she's wrong. This did not make me abandon my ideals. I experienced both happiness and sorrow, but this does not harm the human heart, this does not impoverish a person.

Sonnenschein did not come yesterday. That's when we realize just how much her visits mean to us. We reflect and feel our misery so much more intensely. In despair I sang a song all day about a little butterfly that had to die because he was deprived of the sun. Don't laugh, Teddy.

That is really tragic!

Then I received two letters from my poor mother. She mailed them long ago. It breaks my heart to read her letters. She is so alone and for months has been living with this terrible uncertainty. I know that she spends all her days and nights thinking only of me and praying for me. Her letters reveal her courage and are full of hope, but despite the words, I can feel her pain.

I can't think about this too much because I am falling apart.

Cheers! Another Wednesday has passed; and the news is getting better all the time. I have the same request of you as of Gerd: Can you send me some beautiful poetry? That would make me so happy!

I am so tired every night, I don't know why that is. Probably because I have so much work to do, and I'm so hungry. I don't even feel like talking through the window anymore. Apart from Betty and Tanka in cell #20, my neighbors aren't very interesting.

Dearest Teddy, Sonnenschein was just here. I feel better and can breathe easily again. I've just had a sardine sandwich. Today I can fill up on moldy bread.

Ah, may Gerd's prediction come true and may I soon change my cell in Moabit for a room at Halensee.

You've thought out the matter of your letter to Maria quite wisely and well. But Teddy, is it really necessary to let her know when one of us is killed? She will eventually find out anyway. I still have many, many buttonholes to make, so I end this letter with best wishes and kisses.

Your Kryscha

Alt-Moabit, Berlin
Sometime in October 1943

Dear Ursel and Gerd,

Your letters mean so much to me. How can I thank you for your kind words and good wishes. It feels so good to know that here, not far away, I have good friends who think of me. I used to feel abandoned in this alien land. My country is so far away!

Dear Gerd, I added to your troubles unnecessarily; I am sorry, but at the same time, I am glad. Do you know why? From your letter I realize that you are not indifferent to me. Mimi's death left a void in my life and you have filled it. For that I am very grateful. I thought about her all the time after her death, but they were only sad thoughts, desperate and terrible thoughts.

There was a splendid storm on Saturday; the cell was in complete darkness, and little Lena went to sleep. I got up on the sewing machine to get near the window, smoked a terrific cigarette, and thought about Mimi. Then I was overcome by a longing to be with you in Halensee.

Thank you very much for the pears, which were delicious. The pencils are very useful. I often think now about the time I spent together with Mimi at the Alex. What we used to do just to get our hands on a pencil, and once we got one, it became our greatest treasure. Life was so primitive then, as though we were living on an isolated island. A pencil, scissors, a mirror—these were our treasures. We used scissors to cut the bread, to sharpen our pencils—they were really a universal tool . . . [fragment missing]

I think I once told you about Mimi's neighbor, Henia Weissenstein . . . [end of letter missing]

Alt-Moabit, Berlin
Sometime in October 1943

My dear Teddy,

Thank you for your sweet letter. We feel fabulous. We roar with laughter every night now because, instead of putting handcuffs on both of us, one of us gets these great, thick gloves that can't be removed. It's more comfortable for sleeping, but they are really comical, like a boxer. What a beautiful day it is. We went for a walk after dinner, and there was a little sunshine in the courtyard. You know, I have never had a kiss that thrilled me so much as the warm caress of the sun on my face; it's been so long since I've felt that. I forgot all my cares and felt happy. We long for news of the world. The chains and this whole monkey circus is not important. The only thing that matters is the war and survival. Survival!!

[End missing]

Alt-Moabit, Berlin
Sometime in October 1943

My dear Teddy,

You can no longer expect better paper than this from me.[95] It's just as well that we at least have this boring work and some books. As they told us: "You should be pleased, children, that you don't have to sit all day in chains." I always thought that forcible restraint was used only on dangerous lunatics, but in a Nazi prison, everything is possible.

We spend about a half an hour every evening arguing about what type of handcuffs we'll get for the night. During an alarm there is an inspection every five minutes to check whether we are still in our cell.

Let's hope that the little escapee is in a good hiding place and is having a good laugh at the enraged officers and judges.

It's over a year since I came to Berlin. I regret to this day that I did not jump from the moving train. I would have either died instantly or I'd be free now. Those lazy British and Americans aren't rushing to end this war; they're calmly letting the Russians bleed. [End missing][96]

---

95. The letter was written on a scrap of paper.

96. This was the last letter written from Berlin's Alt-Moabit Prison. Krystyna was transferred to a prison in Halle/Saale in early December. We know from Mrs. Grimpe's (Sonnenschein) correspondence with Marysia Kacprzyk that, in order to ensure that there would be no disturbance, Krystyna was told by the prison director that she was pardoned. But Sonnenschein saw Krystyna when she was being taken from her cell and, noting that she was manacled, realized immediately that the director had lied. After the war, Sonnenschein recalled their last meeting: "She bid me farewell, squeezed my hand, thanked me for everything and smiled—calmly, thoughtfully, and proudly. That's how I will always remember her."

Halle/Saale
December 5, 1943

Beloved parents,

Thank you so much for the lovely things you sent me. I am so deeply touched by your thoughts of me, but I am also sad because I am forbidden to use these things. We have to wear prison uniforms here, but I'm not cold because the radiators are working. I received mail from you a couple of times, Mummy, the last letter dated November 4, with a pretty photo of Kola. Thank you so much for this, my dear sister. Your little one is really marvelous and has such a sweet smile. I often look at his picture.

The parcels that have arrived so far have been given to me. The underwear was included in my things, but please don't send anything else since I get everything that I need here. The only thing I miss are your loving letters, Father, but knowing that everything is well with you, and that your thoughts are with me, I am not discouraged.

I'm afraid that I won't be able to write such long and tiresome letters to you as I did from Berlin. Dear Mummy, I am always so pleased when you write to me about my friends. I am most worried about what's happened to Lena. If you see Mrs. Kacprzyk, thank her for her lovely letter. Has Pani Wanda had any news about Zbyszek?

Christmas is approaching again. The last one was also in jail, but I was with my friends and my dear Mimi. This year I guess I will be completely alone; my thoughts, of course, are with you, particularly you, dear Mummy, because you are so alone. I hope that Halinka and her little one are now in Warsaw. Wish everyone a happy Christmas for me, and special wishes for Pani Wanda, Alinka, and her children.

Once again, thank you for all your letters and parcels, for letting me know you are thinking of me. Don't worry about me; I am strong and in good health.

I end with the hope that you will spend Christmas in peace and kiss you all many times.

Your Krystyna

Many best wishes to Halinka and her family; I would love to play with little Kola someday.

Halle/Saale
January 1, 1944

Dear, kind father,

I only had one wish for Christmas and that was for a letter from you. My Christmas wish came true. It made me so happy that I felt completely contented. I am grateful for your efforts to send me parcels; unfortunately I can't accept them.[97] Thank you for the package of underwear and the Christmas present, which were delivered to me. I would, of course, write long and frequent letters to you if only I could.

Dear parents, is it really true that the officers from Aleja Szucha said that?[98] I won't celebrate until I know for sure—I couldn't bear the disappointment. I thought about you a lot during Christmas. Don't be sad, Mummy, even if they return all the packages that you send me. During the holidays, I saw a Christmas tree, a manger, and I ate my fill. I'm sure you want to know what my life here is like. It's not possible to explain everything; in any case I am not alone. I really miss my friends, and only now do I realize what a priceless gift it is to be among people of equal education with similar perspectives and similar feelings. But I get a lot of wonderful letters. Unfortunately, I am unable to reply to them all—Pani Wanda, Janka, Lena, and Olenka. Please, dear Mummy, thank them all for me. I get a lot of letters from you though they do take a long time to get here, anywhere from four to six weeks. Your Christmas letter is still not here. What did you do at Christmas?

I gather from your letters that life in Warsaw is difficult and dangerous. Sometimes I worry so much about you and others in Warsaw who are so dear to me. I often think about Karol [Szapiro].[99] Where can he be? If he were in Germany, he would find some way of letting his par-

---

97. Regulations at Halle-Saale were very severe.

98. Aleja Szucha was the Gestapo interrogation center in Warsaw, its name taken from the street on which it was located. The Gestapo in Warsaw must have held out some kind of promise to Krystyna's parents, either that they could visit her or that she still might get a reprieve.

99. In a letter written after the war, Marysia Kacprzyk recalled that she had heard while still in prison that Karol had been arrested and shot. Krystyna's parents must have wanted to spare her this news.

ents know. Dear Mummy, please write to Lena; tell her I got her card, I miss her and Sonnenschein terribly, and I'm quite sure that of the two of us, she's more fortunate.

Dearest Father, did you get Gerd Terwiel's address? Berlin, Halensee, Seesenerstrasse 16. I would love to know whether anything terrible happened during the bombing. Unfortunately I can't write to him myself.

Dear Mummy, I need [list of hygienic items]. Print in large letters on the package: "Hygienic supplies." I think they'll let that through. But please don't send any food; there's no point.

I was delighted with Olenka's letter. I am pleased that things are going well for Zbyszek in Berlin, though I doubt that he'll be sent home after he has served his sentence. The Germans need laborers. Ask Pani Wanda to give him my best wishes. Dear Mummy, I am so happy that after all this time you can finally sleep a little more easily. I'm sure this waiting is harder on you than on me. I hope that after all these endless worries I've caused you, I will also bring you some joy.

Best wishes and kisses,

Your Krystyna

Health and happiness to your landlords.

Halle/Saale
[January or February] 1944

Dearest Mummy,

It was so nice to finally get all those belated holiday greetings. Leszek's poem was so moving; I thank him from the bottom of my heart. If I could, I would write long letters to everyone who wrote to me. Please thank Lena and tell her how pleased I was to get her letter and the photo of Teddy. I received some of your packages. Thank Mrs. Kacprzyk for her affectionate letter. She finds it hard to understand that Marysia misses Moabit, but I feel exactly the same way. Despite the very severe conditions, we felt in a way like girls in a very strict boarding school. Mummy, don't worry, I will not break down psychologically. I am not a weak little girl anymore. If one is not a weakling and does not break down at the start, then misfortune makes this person even stronger and more resistant—and this is what happened to me. I get stronger with every day that I am forced to live far from you. Still, I must admit that sometimes I wish I could once again be a child and in your arms.

Dear Alina, thank you so much for your kind thoughts. The few lines you wrote are as lovely as a poem. My conversations with my cell mate are not, I'm afraid, at the same level as ours were. Kisses to you and your little ones.

Dear Pani Wanda, how can I thank you for your kindness? Reading your letters I am able to lose my feeling of loneliness, if only for a while. I feel as though I am with you and not like a fallen leaf, blown by the wind across the earth. I hope today's letter will reassure you. You see, it's just that I have too much time on my hands, and sometimes this shows in my letters, but I am definitely not weakening, not failing in spirit. If that were so, I would blush before all of you. Today's trials are not so important really; when this is all over, we'll quickly forget these difficult times. Please thank everyone who signed the letter—and give my best wishes to the young couple! I envy Niki his work in the forests. Tell him how grateful I am for his faithful friendship.

Dear Mummy, I have to tell you something even though it breaks my heart—you are not permitted to write to me so often!

Best wishes and kisses to all my loved ones in Poland, and you Mummy, most of all.

Your Tina

Halle/Saale
February 27, 1944

My dear parents,

You must be relieved and pleased now that Mr. Greeve[100] has given you a full report that I am in good health and spirits. I think it was awfully kind of him to go to so much trouble for you, Father. I expect

---

100. A German acquaintance of Krystyna's father who visited her in prison.

that you immediately told Mummy every word. I can hardly wait for his visit again and simply don't know how to occupy my mind for the next few long hours. It is really curious that despite the uncertainty of my situation, I am drawn so strongly to study. By the way, it was very pleasant talking to Mr. Greeve about you, Father, and about your work. You are a splendid person, which of course I have always known, but it was lovely to hear it again.

Thank you, dear Mummy, for the package with the sanitary pads and toothpaste. It would be better if you were to write your letters in German. The last letter I got from you is dated January 28th. I want to reassure you again that I am not freezing; I can sit or stand all day in front of the radiators. I'm sure there aren't many people in Warsaw who have such warm rooms. You see, I worry more about you, how things are and will be for you; I'm sure things will get worse in Warsaw. Write me right away and tell me where Niki will be after he is released. I assume he was lucky this time. Sorry, Mummy, but I need another comb. These stupid things probably cost a fortune in Warsaw, but I'm afraid I broke my comb again. I also need some hair clips. My wisdom tooth suddenly decided to act up and caused me a lot of pain, though I did get some tablets for that.

Do you think I don't know what is happening to Lena? I do know. I know exactly. I don't envy her; I'm only glad that she has good friends and good books. It's been four months since I've heard a single word in Polish. I could improve my German I suppose, if my cell mate spoke a decent German instead of *Plattsdeutsch*. Though I do have hope, I can't allow myself to count on winning because there's no further information. I wait, and I am grateful at the end of each day that I am still alive. I think of you, and knowing that I have you, I am actually happy from time to time.

Another winter in prison is soon coming to an end, and one doesn't really feel like dying in the spring. I was sentenced to death on a lovely spring day [April 19, 1943], the kind of day that makes one want to shout with joy, "I'm alive!"

Give my best to all my friends, to dear Pani Wanda, to all the good aunts and everyone who thinks of me. Special regards to faithful old

Krystyna's mother

Miss Tola. Don't worry about me, dear parents. I am well and strong.
Love and kisses,
Your Tina

Halle/Saale
April 23, 1944

Mummy,

You are the best and the most loved Mummy. Every letter and package from you reminds me of this. I know that many people are thinking of me, but you, it's as though you are always with me. Don't you agree? I could lose faith in everything in the world except your love for me. The comb and the sanitary pads arrived; nothing is missing. I love the sweet-smelling soap and the colorful card. Set on my little table during Easter, it cheered up this monotonous cell. You can't imagine how much I liked looking at the little yellow chicks. And at the sight of the little Pascal Lamb, I cried, thinking how much you love me, and I can't even kiss you. Oh, Mummy, sometimes it's not so easy to be brave, especially at moments when I am overcome with homesickness. I'm sure you feel the same way. But we shall overcome this—right, dear, brave Mummy? I received your letters of March 20 and April 9. For two weeks, including the holidays, I was alone. Now I have company again. I've almost finished my Italian book—it's amazing how much I learned in such a short time. I can see the top of a chestnut tree outside my window; what a pleasure to watch the leaves grow and the flowers bud. The sun peeks in after dinner. April 19 marked a year since my death sentence; my friends are probably thinking of me as I am of them. When do you expect Wanek to visit? Where is he now?

Thank you, Janek, for your loving letters. I kiss you, dearest Mummy, and you, Halinka, Janek, and little Kola. Best wishes to Mr. and Mrs. Mierkowski, Leszek, and Janusz.

Beloved, wonderful Father. I received your letter of April 2, and I was so pleased to read your words of praise for my endurance. Admiration from you is doubly pleasing because I know that your standards of behavior are very high. You see, I never forget that I have courageous parents; how I wish that someday I could bring you happiness. You know, there was a time when I wanted everything, but not anymore. I don't miss anyone but you and Mother. I have lived through enough, and I learned a lot about human nature. Now I want only you, my parents, and to walk together with you over the broad meadows at home. And I am fully aware that nobody in the world can help me now, and I must deal with my sorrows myself.

Dear Pani Wanda. Mummy told me such sad news, and I can picture the sorrow in your face. If only I could comfort you. I desperately want to believe that Pan Lucjan [Walc] survived his illness; and perhaps you've had news from Zbyszek by now. It was inevitable that after he served his sentence, he would be transferred to Staatspolizei, and if he is in the Polizeiprasidium, he will only be able to write after four weeks. He might be sent for forced labor, which is infinitely better than to be sent to a camp. If you happen to have a chance, please forward the following words to him.

My dear friend, I fear you may remain behind prison walls for a while yet, though I would be so happy to hear that you had better luck. My dear, good, faithful friend, thinking of you helps me through many difficult hours. It is foolish to be thinking about the future while I remain on the abyss. You know yourself how, often in moments of despair, one must hold on to something strong as a rock just to survive. My rock was your love. Thank you, dear Zbyszek. I worry about you sometimes, but I want to believe that everything will turn out fine. Stay well. All my best,

Your Krystyna

Halle/Saale
May 13, 1944

My beloved parents,

My birthday was wonderful. I experienced so many pleasures all at once that I am once again radiant and happy as I haven't been in a long,

long time. I write this letter full of hope because I want to believe that the most difficult times are behind me, and that before long I will be able to inform you about the final decision concerning my fate. . . .

For some time now I've had more freedom; I've been moved to another cell, and I am permitted to wear my own clothes. On my birthday, everyone here was very kind and warm, and I got my mail—a letter from Father dated May 4, a notebook, a postcard, and a parcel. Thank you so much for the birthday greetings and for everything else. You can imagine, Mummy, how delicious everything was! Your letter of April 27 and the comb were delivered earlier. Now I have two combs, and I'm sure I won't break them again. My hair was really falling out, so I cut it very short. Some people flatter me and say I look like a school-girl, but I'm sure they think I'm a plucked chicken. Please be so kind, Mummy, as to ask Dr. Walc if she has anything that might strengthen my hair and send it to me.[101]

My only care now is for Zbyszek. It's almost certain that he's stuck in another camp. We just have to be patient until he gets a chance to write since 'stapo [the Gestapo] doesn't send any news. I've been hoping for a letter from Pani Wanda, but I guess she's too busy, what with Pan Lucjan being so ill.

For the time being, I am alone in my cell, just me and my books, but I'm not bored—quite the contrary, I'm resting and enjoying the tranquility. I've finished the Italian book, so now I'm going over Italian grammar, which gave me a little trouble. I began writing exercises from the start. Thank you for the news about Lena. It's wonderful that Janek can go to the country again with his family, but I'm sure you will miss your little grandson terribly. Right, Mummy? After all, you must have someone to look after and to spoil!

Ah, Father, how splendid it would be if you could come and visit. Bring your permit from the military court like you did last year; since the death sentence is still hanging over me, you'd better hurry because we don't know how long I'll be here. Maybe it would work! Thank you for your letter, dear Janek. I would have gladly responded to your philosophical observations about happiness if only I had a bigger piece of pa-

---

101. Pani Wanda was a dermatologist.

per. One thing is certain: Happiness as a permanent state is impossible, but even a prisoner condemned to death can experience moments of happiness. As you put it so well, it is, after all, a spiritual matter. There's a beautiful chestnut tree in full bloom outside my window. If you hear a chorus of nightingales singing in Brwinów Park some evening, please think of me. (The chestnut in bloom seems to have put me in a romantic mood.)

Keep your chin up, Mummy! I am well and always thinking of you. Give my best to Pani Wanda and Mrs. Mierkowski.

Kisses to you, Halinka, and little Kola.

Your Tina

Halle/Saale
May 29, 1944

Dear parents,

By now you must have received my letter in which I described my wonderful birthday. Things continue well. If I worry at all now, it is about you; as for myself, I believe that since luck held out for me even in the most dangerous times, so it will continue. I can imagine how you tremble when you hear about the air raids in Germany. Stay calm; during an alarm we all go down to the cellar. I was delighted to get your letter and Janek's card of May 10, as well as a letter from Pani Wanda. I am now certain that Lena's sentence was commuted and she was sent to a penal camp. Ach, Mummy, I had thought that prison had smartened me up, but unfortunately I've decided that I'm a long way from smart. But then, such a conviction must also be a sign of some intelligence.

What are the chances of a visit, dear Father? To be quite honest, I don't think this journey is possible right now. I have a great favor to ask. Please send or bring with you: laundry powder, a small mirror, a washable summer blouse, and some blue—dark blue—clogs. My writing was improving. What a shame my studies had to stop.

Dear Janek, thank you for your letters and your heartfelt interest in me. I hope that Halinka and the little one feel well in their home.

You were asking, Mummy, about my companions, but it is hard to answer that. In the last little while, I frequently changed cells; for the time being I am alone, but I won't be here for long. Give my best to my friends and to all who think of me.

Heartfelt kisses to all,

Your Tina

Halle/Saale

June 18, 1944

My dear parents,

Mr. Greeve's visit was a great pleasure for me. By the time you get this letter, you will have heard about me, about my good spirits, that my work is light, I am not alone, and I manage to hold my head high.

Dear Mummy, Mr. Greeve said that they think Warsaw might be bombed, and I'm quite worried about you. Let's hope our home will be saved.

I received everything that Mr. Greeve brought here. You can imagine how happy I was. I don't know whom I should thank for these lovely and useful things. The shoes with a cork sole fit like a glove and are beautiful. I wore them all day today and had no desire to take them off in the evening; I could sleep in them. The blouse is exactly what I wanted, pretty and practical. The boots are not very useful at the moment. The soap and other toiletries are, as always, much needed.

Dear, sweet Father, it would be so wonderful if you could come! Mr. Greeve once again held out hope. I think that, unlike last year, this time there would be no need for us to keep up appearances while deep inside we querulously wonder: "Will we ever see one another again?" I also received your parcel for Pentecost and also a package of toiletries including the hairbrush, which I really needed. You are an angel, and you think of everything. This is not the best paper in the world, but I hope that you'll be able to make out my writing. Day before yesterday there were two letters (an especially happy day!)—one from Janek dated June 5 and one from Mrs. Kacprzyk. Please thank her. I'm glad that our dear Marysia is in good health and spirits. At present my life is not as lonely as it was during the winter months; since I meet many women at work, I don't have much time to dwell on my problems. The days pass quickly, and every evening I feel happiness, thinking that soon I'll be free.

You ask about my companions. Until recently there was nothing interesting about them, but a couple of weeks ago I found a friend who is very sweet, good, and clever, and we got along very well. Unfortunately we couldn't stay together. I'm sure you understand that this is very hard on me. You know what I'm like; when I find someone who is interesting, my friendship knows no bounds. I'm still like that, so it is depressing to be alone while, not far away, there's a person from whom I could learn something. It would be best if we could stop feeling anything while in jail—or so I sometimes think—but in fact, after you have shed your tears because a friend was killed or taken away, the happiest memories are those of loving friendships. Tears dry, worries are forgotten, but the memory of a beautiful friendship will shine even during our darkest hours. The image of Mimi never fades, and has supported me through many a dark, winter day. The thought of death is made lighter knowing that she has already taken that road. But don't think that these tragic events have made me melancholy. Quite the contrary, I have learned to find joy in life, to think of every beautiful hour as a gift from heaven. Poor Jurek. What a pity to lose such a marvelous youth. And I can't really believe that Karol is no longer alive!

Dear Father, if you can come, please bring me the suitcase, which I will need if I am sent away in a transport. Once again, many, many thanks and best wishes.

Your Krystyna

Krystyna, sometime in 1942

Halle/Saale
June 26, 1944

Beloved parents,

How hard it is to write this last letter. But you must believe me—I am not afraid of death, I do not regret my life. I only think how much sorrow I give you, how you will grieve during the last hours of my life. I want to thank you again for your care and your love, for your unconditional dedication, my dearest Mummy! I can never thank you enough for everything you have done for me, for my joyful, carefree childhood. Don't cry, Mummy, may God ease your pain. I know that you long ago forgave me all the trouble and worry I caused you. I am looking for words that would help me cheer you up, but I can only think of one sentence that Pani Wanda said when she lost Lolek: "God's best-loved die young."

I am completely at peace, believe me, and I will remain serene to the end. My last obligation to Poland and to you is to die bravely.

Beloved Daddy, dearest Mummy, I feel you are with me today, and I am so conscious of my great love for you. I dedicate my last thoughts to you. Be brave! Bid me farewell.

Your Tina[102]

Viel des Edlen hat die Zeit zertrümmert,
Viel des Schonen starb den frühen Tod,
Durch die weichen Blatterkrame schimmert
Seinen Abschied mir das Morgenrot.
Doch um das Verhängnis unbekümmert
Hat vergebans euch die Zeit bedroht
Und es rauscht mir aus der Zweige Wehen:
Alles Grosse muss den Tod bestehen.

Much that was noble, time has destroyed
Much that was beautiful, death has cut short
Through the soft canopy of leaves I see

---

102. End of Krystyna's letters.

The fading shimmer that is dawn's farewell.
Yet heedless you approach your doom
And time threatens you in vain
For the sighing branches whisper to me
All great things must die, to last.[103]

---

103. A German poem written on the back of Krystyna's final letter.

APPENDIX

Letter from a Spokesman of the Military Court

Torgau, July 10, 1944
Zietenkaserne
Telefon 933

Mr. Feliks Wituski
Majątek Brwinów pod Warszawą

Your daughter Krystyna Wituska was sentenced by military court—
1. Senate—on April 19, 1943 and condemned to death for spying, consorting with the enemy, and betraying the state.

The sentence was confirmed on May 21, 1943, and carried out on June 26, 1944, at the Halle-Saale prison following refusal of clemency by the Führer.

Your daughter's last letters are enclosed.

Prepared by:
[signature illegible]
Inspector of Military Court
Signed
Dr. Fleischmann

Letter from Mrs. Hedwig Grimpe

Letter to Mrs. Wituska written by Helga Grimpe on behalf of her mother, Sonnenschein. Krystyna's mother had written to Mrs. Grimpe thanking her for the care and affection she had given her daughter while she was at Alt-Moabit Prison.

Berlin
December 12, 1946

Honorable lady,

I can only assure you without exaggeration what happiness I felt reading your first words to me. You lifted from me a very heavy burden. How often I wanted to write to you! But every letter ended the same way: in the fire, torn up, destroyed because of the awful conviction that, in your eyes, they may seem to be lies and hypocrisy in view of the fact that it was Germans who tormented Krystyna and pursued her to her death. I am German and so I can't help but feel responsible for all the deeds and atrocities committed by my nation. Therefore Krysia's death, as all the others, will always be for me a terrible guilt. Please don't thank me! For what? What could I do for Tina—or, in fact, what did I do for Tina?

I have much more to be grateful for to Krystyna than she to me. Her courage and that of her friends proved to me that I must honor the Polish nation, all Polish people.

I feel an obligation to go to Halle-Saale to see if I can get more information about Tina. As soon as I get permission and documents to enable me to take the trip, I will go there, and, of course, I will not fail to inform you of everything that I can.

I want to assure you, that I will do anything to earn your respect, and if possible, your friendship. I will try to do everything possible so that you will be able to believe that there are better Germans.

In this spirit, I send you my best wishes and remain ever in your service,

Helga Grimpe

Appendix

Family and Friends: An Annotated List

RITA ARNOULD
Executed August 19, 1943, at Plotzensee.

CEZARA DICKSTEIN
Transported to Alexanderplatz with Krystyna, then sent to Ravensbruck.

HELENA (LENA, LENKA) DOBRZYCKA
Arrested in mass arrest (43 persons) of underground members in Gdansk (Danzig). Condemned to death in Berlin, but sentence commuted. Sent to Stutthof concentration camp in February 1944, escaped from forced march during the evacuation of the camp in March 1945. Of the remaining 42 arrested with her, 39 were executed, one was sent to Auschwitz where he died, one survived Fordon Prison, and one is unaccounted for.

MONIKA DYMSKA
Guillotined June 25, 1943, age 25, at Plotzensee Prison, Berlin. Her father was killed at the Oranienburg concentration camp; her mother survived the Ravensbruck concentration camp for women; her sister, Irena, and brother, Mieczysław, survived imprisonment and torture at Fort VII in Torun.

JANEK
Identified only by his first name, an escapee from Auschwitz, removed from Alt-Moabit and never heard from again.

CHRISTINA JANEVA, "TANKA"
The Bulgarian prisoner in the cell beside Krystyna. She was executed at Plotzensee.

OLGA (OLENKA) JĘDRKIEWICZ
Transported to Alexanderplatz with Krystyna, and her cell mate at Alt-Moabit. Sent to penal camp, Witten-Annen.

Appendix

WIESŁAWA JEZIERSKA
Guillotined at age 31 at Plotzensee, March 9, 1943, with her colleague, Olga Kamińska.

MARIA (MARYSIA) KACPRZYK
Arrested with Krystyna, transferred from Pawiak Prison in Warsaw to Alexanderplatz, then to Alt-Moabit in Berlin. Sentenced then to eight years at Fordon Prison.

OLGA KAMIŃSKA
Sentenced after giving birth to a son, who was taken to a German orphanage. She was executed at Plotzensee on March 9, 1943, age 21. Worked as a courier/escort taking escaped POWs across the Yugoslav border. The seven women couriers in this group were all executed.

WANDA KAMIŃSKA
Arrested with Krystyna, transferred from Pawiak to Alexanderplatz and then Alt-Moabit. Sentenced to three years in the penal camp Witten-Annen.

STEFANIA PRZYBYŁ
Escaped from Alt-Moabit. Her sister, Helena Mackowiak, was guillotined at Plotzensee on October 17, 1943, age 36; her mother and another sister were subsequently arrested.

MARTA RACHEL
Friend of Stefania Przybył's, executed.

KAROL SZAPIRO
Krystyna's beloved Jewish friend, arrested at a railway station and shot; details unknown. Fate of parents unknown.

MARIA (MIMI) TERWIEL AND HANS HELMUT HIMPEL
Guillotined at Plotzensee.

ZBYSZEK WALC
Prisoner of war, October 25, 1939, in Stalag II Neubrandenburg. Turned over to the Gestapo for forced labor in March 1942. Arrested in

the fall of 1942, trial at Alexanderplatz, then Alt-Moabit Prison. Sent to concentration camps—first Sachsenhausen, then Buchenwald. Burned to death in a barn along with other prisoners during a forced march in the last weeks of the war.

WANDA WĘGIERSKA
Arrested April 1942, tortured in Łódź, Warsaw, and Alexanderplatz. Guillotined April 25, 1943, age 24. Father, Edward, arrested October 13, 1939, in Łódź, deported to Sachsenhausen-Oranieneburg where he died in May 1940. Mother imprisoned in Łódź; brother killed in Auschwitz August 12, 1942; sister and sister-in-law survived Auschwitz.

Alina, Krystyna's aunt, and her children survived, although her husband was killed in battle. Krystyna's parents, sister Halina, her husband, Janusz, and their child, Kola, also survived.